ORCHIDS

ORCHIDS

MICHAEL TIBBS

NEW
HOLLAND

This paperback edition first published in 2010 by

New Holland Publishers Ltd

London | Sydney | Auckland | South Africa

www.newhollandpublishers.com

| 86-88 Edgware Road, London W2 2EA, United Kingdom | Unit 1, 66 Gibbes Street, Chatswood, NSW 2067, Australia | 218 Lake Road, Northcote, Auckland, New Zealand | 80 McKenzie Street, Cape Town, South Africa 8001 |

ISBN 978 1 84773 882 0

Publishing managers: Simon Pooley, Claudia dos Santos

Commissioning editor: Alfred LeMaitre

Editor: Gill Gordon

Design: PETALDESIGN

Cover design: Helen Henn

Illustrator: Steven Felmore

Production: Myrna Collins

Consultant: Dr Phillip Cribb

Reproduction by Pica Digital Pte Ltd

Printed and bound in Malaysia by Times Offset (M) Sdn Bhd

HALF TITLE PAGE *Phalaenopsis* Acapulco used in an arrangement.
PREVIOUS PAGE The lip of an *Odontoglossum*.
OPPOSITE Orchids growing in a protected garden setting.

CONTENTS

UNDERSTANDING ORCHIDS

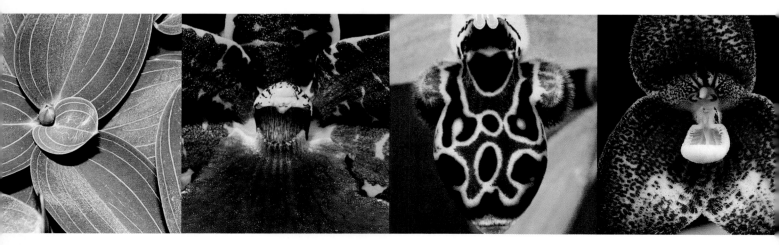

ORCHID HYBRIDS

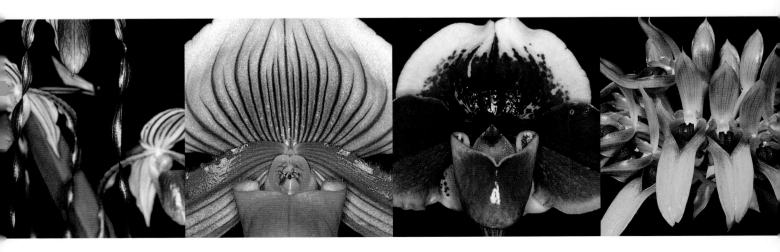

FOREWORD

Growing orchids has never been more popular. It is truly an international pastime but, strangely, growing orchids is still considered by many to be difficult and expensive. Nothing could be further from the truth. Modern propagation methods – often growing orchids in the laboratory from seed or multiplying the growing tip of a choice orchid in a nutrient medium (meristemming) that encourages the growth of many small plants – has brought tropical orchids within the price range of many people throughout the world. While some orchids are truly difficult to grow, with very exacting demands for their culture, most orchids that can be purchased in nurseries, supermarkets and florists are easy to grow providing that the instructions on the label are followed. Furthermore, orchids are such good value. Many flower for extended periods – six months' continuous flowering from a moth orchid is not uncommon.

Orchids are rewarding subjects for both the amateur and for the serious grower. Whether you grow them on the kitchen window-sill, bathroom, garden or glasshouse, there are orchids that will suit your purpose. Growers often specialize early on – many stay with a particular group of orchids, such as slipper orchids or Masdevallias, while others adopt a more catholic approach and fill their glasshouse with a kaleidoscope of colour. With increasing experience, a grower can graduate from the easy moth, jewel or slipper orchids to the more demanding Dracula, Odontoglossum or terrestrial orchids. There will be something in the family to satisfy everyone's taste. If you like large, showy flowers, try Cattleya or Laelia; if you like miniature orchids then Pleurothallis or Bulbophyllum might suit you better. If you lack a glasshouse, there are plenty of orchids that thrive outdoors and will brighten your garden throughout the spring and summer months.

There are also orchids to suit everyone's pocket: orchid prices have never been so low. In the 19th century orchid growing was a rich man's hobby – now you can now feel just like a Victorian millionaire on a mere fraction of the outlay!

Mike Tibbs, the author of this guide book to growing orchids, is one of the most widely travelled and experienced orchid specialists. Few orchid growers have his breadth of experience, achieved during his career on four continents. He has managed one of the best-known orchid collections in Britain, has worked in both Japan and the USA with major breeders, and has run his own nurseries in South Africa. This book reflects his wealth of knowledge of orchids, from cultivation techniques to plant breeding and showing. In this book he provides a simple, straightforward and well-illustrated guide to orchids and their cultivation, one that will no doubt increase the number of people taking up orchid-growing as a deeply satisfying and rewarding past-time.

Dr Phillip Cribb
Honorary Research Fellow at
the Royal Botanic Gardens, Kew

OPPOSITE *Miltoniopsis* (Charlesworthii x Colwell). Some Miltoniopsis species have large open flowers which glow in the dim light just before dawn, when they are believed to be pollinated by nocturnal bees.

Understanding orchids

AN INTRODUCTION TO ORCHIDS

The Orchidaecae are one of the largest families in the plant kingdom, consisting of over 25,000 documented species, some 800 subspecies and, at recent count, around 110,000 registered hybrids. Most species occur in the subtropical and tropical regions of Asia, South and Central America, but this diverse and adaptable family of flowering plants is found all around the globe, except for the polar regions and most arid deserts. Certain orchids live high in the rainforest canopy clinging to the branches of a host tree, some grow on the forest floor, while others have adapted to living in rock crevices, or in decaying organic matter.

While climate change and human interference in natural habitats are contributing to the decline and, in some cases, extinction of certain orchid species, exploration in the depths of the rain forests and previously unexplored parts of Asia and South America are revealing exciting new discoveries. Furthermore, new hybrids are being produced all the time.

Orchid flowers come in a wide array of shapes, sizes, colours and fragrances, that often challenge easy identification. Among the smallest are the pinhead-sized flowers of the miniature moss orchid (*Bulbophyllum globuliforme*), while the tiger orchid (*Grammatophyllum speciosum*), the largest orchid plant in the world, produces between 60–100 single flowers up to 15cm (6in) across on stems up to 2–3m (6.5–10ft) long. Flowers may be blousy and frilly, or long and slender, and are produced as a single stately bloom or in a neat row atop an arching stalk. They can be delicately striped, boldly spotted or lightly dappled, sometimes in magnificently intricate patterns. Colours range from pearly whites, pale green, pink and yellow to rich shades of magenta, orange or blue. The deepest red shades are sometimes mistaken for black, but there is no true black orchid.

The flowers emit scents that range from delicately sweet to sharply spicy, musty to putrid. The flowers of *Encyclia fragrans* produce a strong honey-vanilla fragrance, *Paphiopedilum malipoense* emits a strong fragrance that can be described as rich raspberry. Less alluring is *Bulbophyllum graveolens*, which smells like rotting meat.

The leaves, too, vary in size, shape and markings. Some species such as the jewel orchid (*Ludisia discolor*) are prized more for their spectacular foliage than their flowers. Others, such as *Microcoelia exilis* have no leaves at all and are intriguing for their tangle of flowering stems and visible roots.

PREVIOUS PAGES (MAIN IMAGE) *Phalaenopsis stuartiana* 'Grange Gold' AM/AOS.

THE CLASSIFICATION OF ORCHIDS

Scientific plant names are subject to rules laid down in the International Code of Botanical Nomenclature (ICBN), administered by the International Association for Plant Taxonomy (IAPT) and subject to revision every five years.

Unlike most plants, which are described using just the genus and species, many orchids are hybrids and need a hybrid name. So, in addition to being governed by the ICBN regulations, which apply only to plants found in the wild, orchids are also subject to the International Code of Nomenclature for Cultivated Plants developed for man-made hybrids. The codes were developed to ensure that no two orchids ever have the same name; all orchid names are governed by these codes. Before a new species can be accepted, a scientific name must be described in the prescribed way in Latin and a type specimen cited. The type specimen is usually the first introduction and is often pressed for herbarium collections. To be accepted, the name must be published in a distributed journal, book or some other recognized publication.

When describing an orchid, the species or genus is followed by a unique name, usually given by the describing botanist. This may represent a character-istic of the flower or plant, its location, or the name of the founder, and is written in Latinized form, even when derived from another language (for example *Cymbidium* Cherry Blossom).

The first part of the scientific label is the generic name or genus, i.e. *Paphiopedilum* (generic names all start with a capital letter). The second part is the specific scientific adjective or epithet that identifies the species within its genus. When a generic name is repeated in a sentence or list it is abbreviated to just the initial capital letter, followed by a fullstop (e.g. *Paphiopedilum insigne*, *P. rothschildianum*). Specific epithets, like *insigne*, are always written in lower case. The first two parts of the name are often followed by a third, frequently abbreviated, that represents the name of the botanist who first described the species.

Botanical classification is done according to a hierarchical system. This means that each higher rank, such as an order or family (see diagram below), includes a number of subordinate groups that share certain characteristics. A family, for example, consists of one or more genera, each having more in common with one another than with the genera of other families. With genera it's the same, but they comprise one or more related species.

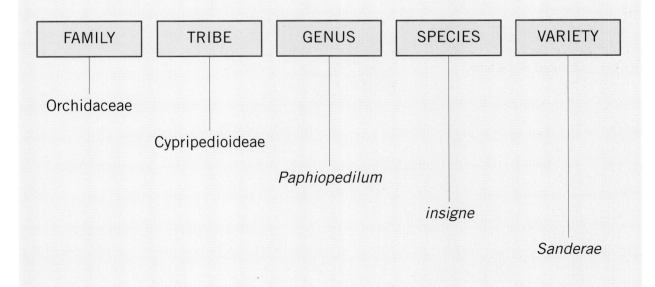

| FAMILY | TRIBE | GENUS | SPECIES | VARIETY |

Orchidaceae

Cypripedioideae

Paphiopedilum

insigne

Sanderae

STRUCTURE OF THE PLANT

Orchids are differentiated from other plants by three characteristics that make them unique: their flowers, reproductive parts and roots.

THE FLOWER

Orchid flowers are uniquely zygomorphic or bilaterally symmetrical: dividing each flower on the vertical plane, and the vertical plane only, will produce two identical halves (other flowers may be divided on any plane to produce two mirror images). The flowers of orchids come in many sizes, colours, textures and shapes, from magnificently beautiful to curiously bizarre. Within this vast array, the flowers share a common structure – they are made up of three sepals and three petals arranged in a pinwheel or whorl shape, and a reproductive structure called the column.

Sepals and petals

These form the outer and inner ring of the flower respectively. The sepals sometimes resemble petals in colour and texture and are generally equal in size; in some species the uppermost (dorsal) sepal may be slightly larger and more prominent than the lower ones.

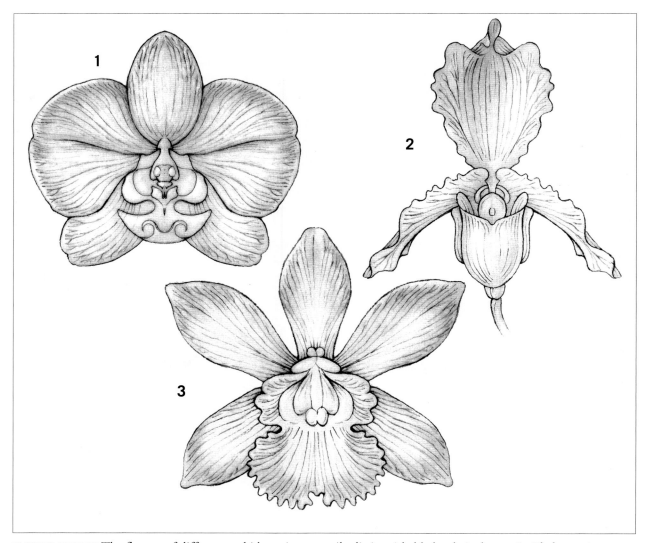

FLOWER SHAPES The flowers of different orchid species are easily distinguishable by their shapes. 1. *Phalaenopsis*; 2. *Paphiopedilum*; 3. *Cattleya*.

The two lower (lateral) sepals, may appear fused in some species, but close examination will usually reveal their point of separation. Sepals are usually less flamboyant than petals, but in some species, such as *Masdevallia*, they have developed into the main attraction of the flower. One petal, most often positioned at the bottom of the flower, is modified into an ingeniously engineered and often spectacularly formed segment called the lip (labellum). Petals and lip are generally, but not always, larger than the sepals.

The lip

The lip can be trumpet-shaped, fringed, curved, elongated, or formed like a little pouch. It may be striped or speckled, vibrantly or softly hued. In many orchids the lip is the largest and most ornate feature of the flower, in others it is small and unremarkable. In some species, the lip is fixed and performs its function with decorative lures.

Its purpose is to act as a landing-pad for prospective pollinators such as bees, luring them to the flower with extravagant shapes and colouring. To this end, it may appear as a single, or multilobed structure, adorned with tufts of hair, bumps or ridges. In other orchids the lip is engineered to play a more active role in effecting pollination, acting as a trap to prevent the pollinator from leaving the flower until it has collected or deposited pollen.

Many orchid species depend upon a specific pollinator for reproduction; some rely on flies, others on bees, gnats, moths, butterflies, or even hummingbirds. The lip is specifically designed to facilitate this selective pollination process. In many Bulbophyllums, for example, the lip forms a sensitive hinged swing that propels the visiting insect towards the pollen. In the genus Paphiopedilum, one of a group known as slipper orchids, the lip forms a slipper-like pouch that traps the insect until pollination is complete. Several orchid species store nectar in a tube or spur at the back of the lip where it can only be reached by a pollinator with a tongue or other proboscis suited to the length of the spur. Examples are *Aerangis* and *Angraecum sesquipedale*, the comet orchid, which possess a long nectar-filled spur. In most orchids, the lip is positioned at the bottom of the flower, a process known as resupination. In bud

form the lip is positioned at the top. As the bud matures, it moves 180° and the lip moves to the bottom. A few species, like *Encyclia cochleata*, are non-resupinate, i.e. the lip remains at the top of the flower and performs its function in a different way, by trapping the pollinator underneath its hood.

THE COLUMN (REPRODUCTIVE PARTS)

Most conventional flowers contain both a male organ (the stamen, which contains pollen grains) and a female organ (the pistil, with a stigma that receives pollen grains), and are thus bisexual. Orchids are unique in that their male and female organs are fused into the waxy, tubular structure at the centre of the flower called the column.

At the top of the column, pollen grains form golden yellow waxy masses called pollinia, contained in the anther cap. Depending upon the species, there may between two and eight pollinia. These are attached to a sticky disk and held together by fine threads and protected by an anther-cap, located at the very tip

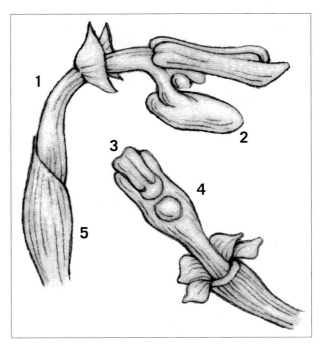

THE REPRODUCTIVE PARTS 1. Ovary; 2. Stigma; 3. Anther; 4. Column; 5. Bract.

of the column. The pollinia represent the male part of the flower.

Just back from the tip, on the underside of the column, is the stigma or stigmatic surface. Very sticky and highly receptive to pollen, the stigmatic surface represents the female part of the flower.

The male and female segments of the column are separated by a section of tissue, the rostellum, which forms a beak-like structure above the anther-cap. The rostellum prevents self-pollination of the flower and also secretes a glue-like liquid that helps to ensure pollen grains stick to visiting pollinators.

A few orchids, such as Catasetums, are single-sexed, with male and female flowers being produced from time to time, but these are exceptional.

THE ROOTS

In the plant world, roots serve two basic functions: to anchor the plant in the ground and to absorb moisture and nutrients. This is true of orchids as well, but there are a few different distinguishing characteristics. Orchid roots are generally thicker and appear as individual strands as opposed to the fine, prolific mesh of roots found in most other plants. The fragile inner core of the root is protected by a thick spongy layer of greyish-white protective tissue called the velamen. The velamen is made up of air-filled pockets of dead cells making the tissue highly absorbent. The outer layer is often covered in fine hair-like projections similar to the absorptive roots of other plants. Throughout an orchid's life, new roots are produced as the old ones die off.

This *Phragmipedium* flower clearly shows the hair-fringed staminode that protects the pollinia. The staminode acts as a target for prospective pollinators – as they try to land on it, they fall into the pouch below. When they emerge they carry pollen masses which can be deposited on the stigmatic surface of the next flower to be visited, thus fertilizing it.

Microcoelia exilis – a leafless orchid that derives nutrition from decaying leaves, humidity and from the rain.

This well-rooted Cymbidium has adapted to being cultivated in a pot.

Underground roots

The underground roots of terrestrial orchids (those that prefer a ground-level habitat), perform the conventional functions of anchoring and absorbing moisture and nutrients from the soil. These plants may have slender absorptive roots in addition to the thick velamen-covered ones. Some species also develop one or more underground tubers, the fleshy bulb-shaped growths that store moisture and nutrients for the plant during its dormant period, after which new growth appears from the tubers.

Aerial roots

Most orchids are epiphytic plants, which means they grow on trees or sometimes rocks. Thick, strong, aerial roots with super absorption capacity allow the plant to attach securely to a host tree and virtually 'live on air'. Aerial roots have a green growing tip that is extremely fragile and indicates that the root is actively growing. Aerial roots may grow to several metres in length and are often flattened to provide a firmer grip on the host. An important point is that the aerial roots absorb all the required moisture and nutrients from the air. The host tree acts primarily as support base rather than food source.

In certain orchid species that shed their leaves for part of the year or are entirely leafless, such as *Chilochistra parishii* and related species, the roots contain the chlorophyll required for photosynthesis, the process by which green plants use solar energy to convert water and carbon dioxide into nutrients.

In epiphytic orchids with a sympodial growth habit (see page 19), roots grow from the base of the pseudobulb and the connecting rhizome. In monopodial epiphytes (see page 20), the roots may grow at regular intervals along the stem, or only from the part of the stem just below the leaves.

Some roots take very interesting forms. For example, *Ansellia* produce side roots with a spiky appearance that grow straight up from the main root, around the base of the plant. Perhaps this unusual growth protects the plant, or helps to catch organic debris to provide additional nutrients for the plant. Whatever the purpose of this bizarre growth habit, it is a feature unique to orchids.

THE LEAVES

Orchid leaves are as diverse as their flowers – they may be cylindrical or broad, paper-thin or thick and succulent, minute or one metre (3ft) or more in length.

Most leaves come in shades of green, blue and grey, but a special group known as the jewel orchids produce leaves in shades of grey, green, red or brown, marked with silver, bronze and copper-toned patterns that are unique in the plant world. Other orchid species are completely leafless.

Leaves may grow in a fan shape from the base of the plant, or alternately up the plant stem at intervals ranging from a few to several centimetres. In many ways, the orchid leaf is the best reflection of a plant's adaptation to its environment. For example, many species of Vanda grow in shaded environments and their broad, flat or pinnate leaves are designed for maximum exposure to sunlight.

Brassavolas, which grow in the tropical regions of South and Central America, have fleshy pencil-shaped leaves (known as terete). Their form exposes minimal surface area to the harsh tropical sun and their fleshy substance holds moisture.

The elegantly striped leaves of *Ludisia discolor*, also known as the jewel orchid.

GROWTH HABITS

Within the bewildering complexity of forms presented by the orchid family, the growth habits of the plants may be generally classified into two distinct categories: sympodial growth and monopodial growth.

SYMPODIAL GROWTH

Most orchids have what is called a sympodial form of growth. The main stem of the plant grows horizontally along the surface of support, with branches growing laterally from this main stem from where it produces its flowers. As flowers die the main stem produces new leads, and new growth sprouts from or next to the previous one.

Most sympodial orchids produce thick bulb-like stems called pseudobulbs, (from the Greek word *pseudes* meaning 'false'), so named because they resemble flower bulbs which, in fact, they are not; true flower bulbs are a complete plant in a package. A tulip bulb, for example, contains a tulip in miniature, along with all the nutrients the plant requires to sprout, grow and flower in the appropriate season.

Pseudobulbs, which store moisture and nutrients for the plant, grow along a fibrous part of the rootstock called the rhizome. In some species, such as Coelogyne or Bulbophyllum, where the pseudobulbs are produced at intervals of approximately 3–4cm (1½ –2in), the rhizome is visible. In other species, such as Cymbidiums, the rhizome acts as a very short thread, connecting pseudobulbs that appear to grow in bunches.

Pseudobulbs come in many sizes and shapes. Dendrobium pseudobulbs can be long and thin or short and squat and may grow up to 2m (6ft) in length, whereas Cymbidium pseudobulbs are mostly egg-shaped and may grow from a few millimetres to over 15cm (6in).

Leaves, flower stems and flowers all develop out of the new growth from the pseudobulb. The new growth will appear from the bulb, fresh leaves will emerge and a new bulb will form along the rhizome. After supporting the new growth, the existing pseudobulb, now nearly depleted, generally goes dormant and becomes what is called a back bulb. In this phase, the new growth will exploit the last energy resources stored in the back bulb until, when these are exhausted, the back bulb shrivels and dies.

A few sympodial orchids do not produce pseudobulbs. Many species of Paphiopedilum that grow in China, India and Southeast Asia where moisture levels are high, grow stout shoots from the base of the plant. As the leaves and shoots die, new growth appears from the existing base. Their thick fleshy roots hold whatever moisture reserves they require.

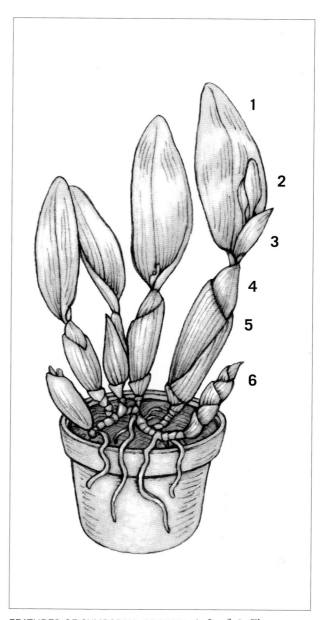

FEATURES OF SYMPODIAL GROWTH 1. Leaf; 2. Flower buds; 3. Sheath; 4. Pseudobulb. 5. Bract; 6. New growth.

MONOPODIAL GROWTH

In contrast to sympodial orchids that grow horizontally, monopodial orchids grow vertically, with some species reaching quite remarkable heights (many species of Vanda, for instance can grow to several metres tall). Flower stems emerge alternately along a main stem between the leaves. The leaves, which also grow alternately on either side of the stem, may be narrow or broad, widely spaced or compact.

Despite some rather dramatic variations in form, the primary growth feature of monopodial orchids is that new growth develops out of the old growth. New shoots can grow from the end bud of an old shoot, and leaves and flowers are then produced along the new stem.

Monopodial orchids have no pseudobulbs, but tend to have succulent leaves in which they store nutrients and moisture.

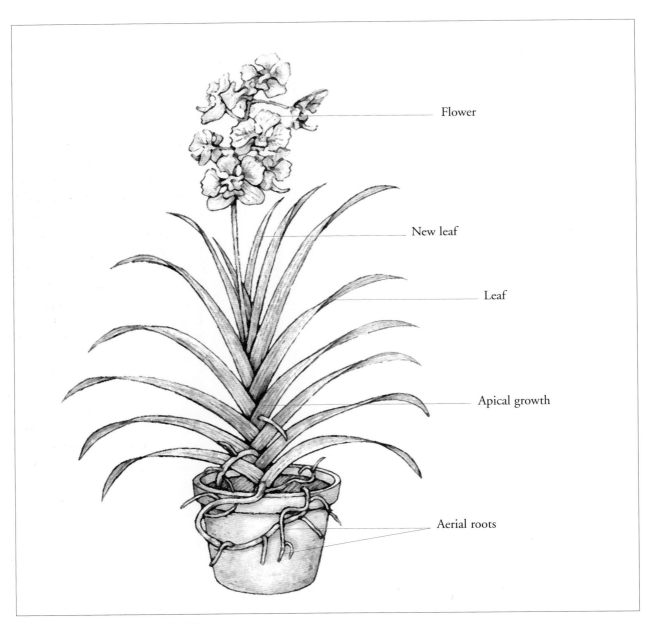

Flower

New leaf

Leaf

Apical growth

Aerial roots

FEATURES OF MONOPODIAL GROWTH

HABITAT

Although a few orchid species survive in bogs, marshes and similar damp conditions, orchids are primarily classified according to their preference for growing on trees, in the ground, on rocks or on piles of organic decaying material. They are divided into three main groups: epiphytes, terrestrials and lithophytes.

In certain circumstances there is crossover among the growing habits of these groups. An epiphytic orchid that falls from a tree may grow in the ground below if the conditions are suitable. Likewise, a terrestrial orchid growing near the base of a tree may grow on the trunk and adopt an epiphytic lifestyle. Either will grow on rocks if the opportunity arises and if there is sufficient moisture and nutrients to support growth.

EPIPHYTES

The word epiphyte is derived from the Greek terms *epi* (meaning on top, or above) and *phyte* (meaning plant). The vast majority of orchids are epiphytic. Most orchids grow in tropical and subtropical areas. They represent many of the most spectacular and widely cultivated orchid species.

Epiphytic orchids grow on host trees supported by the trunk and thick lower branches, or perched securely on small twigs in the very top of the canopy. Epiphytes cling to the host tree with very strong roots and take advantage of moisture and nourishing organic debris that may be caught in the crevices of the bark. Additional moisture and nutrients are absorbed from the humid tropical air (air movement is a key requirement for epiphytic orchids).

Although epiphytic orchids are not parasitic, the plants do fully exploit the variety of micro-climates offered by an aerial lifestyle. Orchids that prefer shade or moderate light grow on the trunk or lower branches of the tree, while species that crave direct light and ventilation position themselves at the top of their host. Some species select specific hosts for the type of support or shelter they offer and may even be found growing in a particular position, such as on just one side of the tree.

Trydactyle tricuspis – an African epiphyte orchid growing in the wild.

A large stand of *Eulophia angolensis*, a terrestrial orchid indigenous to tropical and southern Africa, growing in the damp area near the sea in KwaZulu Natal, South Africa.

TERRESTRIALS

Terra is the Latin word for earth, so it is logical that terrestrial orchids grow in the ground. In fact, this type of orchid has a remarkable ability to adapt to growing conditions that range from damp forest floors and boggy ravines to sandy dunes and semi-arid deserts.

The roots of these orchids produce tubers that may lie just below the soil surface or deep underground. They store nutrient-laden moisture and provide reserves for the plant during dry spells. Many terrestrial orchids are deciduous: flowers and leaves fade in winter and the plants become dormant underground. When the next growing season begins, new growth appears as a single leafy stem topped by one or more flowers. Terrestrials can grow as solitary individual plants or in impressive colonies, sometimes numbering in the hundreds.

LITHOPHYTES

Generally found in tropical regions, lithophytes take their name from the Greek word for stone. These orchids grow on exposed rock, sometimes making their home on high outcrops. In the manner of epiphytes, their strong roots absorb moisture and nutrients from the air, with additional supplies found in rock crevices where moss and organic debris collects. These orchids often have fleshy leaves or succulent pseudobulbs which store moisture and allow the plant to tolerate prolonged dry spells.

AN ORCHID'S LIFE CYCLE

The life cycle of an orchid is much like that of any other plant: seed is produced and germinates, seedlings mature, the plants flower and then reproduce.

POLLINATION

The act of pollination sets in motion a chemical reaction that channels the plant's resources into seed production. The wilting bloom of the flower is the first signal that this process has commenced. When pollination is completed, the sepals and petals begin to shrivel and die. Such a reaction is not at all uncommon among flowering plants, but orchids exhibit extraordinary differences in life cycle habits.

Within a species, the flowering time period may vary significantly after pollination. Equally, the duration of the complete cycle, from pollination to fertilization and the release of seed, may take anywhere from nine to 14 months, with a few exceptions.

SEED FORMATION AND GERMINATION

Seeds forms in a capsule behind the flower after pollination has taken place. A common feature among most orchid species is their prolific seed production. The average orchid seed capsule contains multitudes of seeds that appear as very fine, pale yellow dust. Depending on the species, it can take from a few weeks to almost a year for the seed to mature. (Disas take as little as six weeks, whereas Cymbidiums and Cattleyas need up to 12 months to mature.)

As most orchid species are epiphytic (see page 21), a heavy seed would fall from the tree and land on the ground, which is not where epiphytes prefer to grow. However, a small, delicate seed is easily airborne and stands a better chance of landing in a hospitable spot; perhaps in the crook of a branch among leafy debris, or in a moss-covered crevice on the trunk. Terrestrial orchids have specific soil requirements, but dispersing a copious quantity of seed increases their chances of

Hawk moth (Sphingidae) pollinating a *Platanthera*. After pollination the seed pod will form. It can take between six weeks and twelve months for the seed to mature, depending on the type of orchid.

propagation, particularly considering the highly specific conditions required for successful germination. For the extraordinarily large number of seeds produced and dispersed, only a small percentage actually land in a suitable growing environment.

Orchid seeds lack endosperm, a substance found in the seeds of plants such as peas and beans, which provides the energy required for germination. Unless germinated under laboratory conditions, orchid seeds require a fungus in order to germinate. A *mycorrhiza* is a natural fungus, often a common soil or epiphytic fungus. Only the seeds which are dispersed near enough to the mycorrhizal fungus will germinate (without it, the seed would simply not germinate). Initially, the fungus invades the seed as a parasite in search of sustenance

but, before it becomes destructive, the embryo inhibits the activity of the potentially destructive invader. Once contained, the fungus provides the embryo with the nutrients it requires to germinate and mature (a process that may take three to five years). So begins a symbiotic relationship between fungus and orchid that continues for the life of the plant. The fungus lives in the orchid roots, assisting in the absorption and processing of moisture and nutrients.

Soon after landing in a suitable growing environment, some evidence of germination will appear. Months later, the plant produces a single identifiable leaf, with leaves and roots becoming visible as it develops into a recognizable plant.

Phragmipedium *Grande*

THE LIFE CYCLE OF A CATTLEYA

The cycle begins when pollination has taken place, either naturally by an insect, or artificially by hand. After pollination a seed will form, usually taking around nine months to mature.

Seed is dispersed by the wind in nature; in laboratory conditions it is harvested and flasked. After germination, the young seedlings take about four to five years to mature and flower for the first time, depending on conditions in the greenhouse. From the first time the plant flowers it is able to reproduce. In a laboratory the seed will form protocorms, green masses of tissue that turn into small plants. When these are big and strong enough in the flask, the seedlings can be planted into community pots. They have to be potted on through to maturity.

Day 1: Pollinia is deposited manually on the stigmatic surface of the column where pollen grows to form a tubular-shaped glutinous mass.

The pollen tubes begin moving through a central duct in the column towards the ovary that is located in the stem just behind the flower. This section of the ovary begins to swell, forming an oval shaped seed capsule.

(NB: remember to label the pollinated plant, listing the information of both parents and the date the cross was made.)

Months 2–5: By the end of month two, the pollen tubes fill the ovary completely, encasing the placenta and the unfertilized ovules that begin to develop over the next few months as they prepare for fertilization. By the end of the fifth month, each pollen tube has penetrated a small orifice in each ovule – fertilization takes place.

Months 7–12: Over the next seven months, the seed capsule ripens and turns from pale green to yellow or brown. The precise duration of this part of the process varies according to temperature and other environmental conditions. It also varies between species. At the end of approximately one year the pod dries and begins to split along its lateral ridges, gradually releasing seed.

SCENT AND COLOUR

Many orchid blooms are fragrant. Some species emit pleasantly sweet odours with hints of chocolate or coconut, while others produce musty fragrances. Still others are much less attractive, producing putrid odours. Within this range, fragrance is a very effective method of selectively attracting pollinators.

Orchids produce fragrance through special glands, usually located on the lip. Since this is an energy-intensive process for the plant, the production and release of scent is specifically timed to the daily habits of the desired pollinator. For example, *Cattleya luteola* – a bee-pollinated flower – emits a sweet fragrance in the early morning when bees are at their most active, but at night it has no scent at all. Conversely, most *Angraecum* species, which are pollinated by moths, emit very little fragrance during the day but intensify at night when moths are most active.

With their shortsighted, specialized sense of vision, insects are the primary players in orchid pollination. Many experts think that scent is a more powerful long-distance lure than colour, but the colours and often intricate patterns of many orchids are highly effective cues that lead prospective pollinators into the flower to complete their task.

Some Cattleyas have gold striped markings on the lip, leading directly to the column and a store of nectar. These markings act as a visual aid for visiting wasps and bees. The brilliant white flowers of *Brassavola nodosa* are a beacon for nocturnal moths who can only distinguish between light and dark. The graceful flowers of *Psychopsis papilio*, one of the commonly named butterfly orchids, come in shades of yellow, orange and brown, with a shape resembling a butterfly, an impression enhanced by the gentle motion of the long-stemmed flowers swaying in the breeze.

Angraecum stella-africae provides a sweet gardenia perfume in the evenings when it will most likely be pollinated in the wild.

Calanthe Takane produces a jasmine-like fragrance. Many white flowers are night-scented to attract their nocturnal pollinators.

MIMICRY

The term 'mimicry' refers to the process by which individuals of different species have evolved to resemble one another. In the case of orchids many species have developed an intricate combination of scent, colour and structure designed to mimic, and therefore entice, specific pollinators.

The flower *Ophrys sphegodes* presents a convincing imitation of a specific type of female bee. The male bees of this species hatch several weeks before the females

Ophrys kotschyi shows a fine example of a lip that is designed to attract pollinators.

The extravagantly patterned flowers of *Ophrys sphegodes* – a bumblebee impersonator.

and the bloom of the flower is timed to coincide precisely with this period. As the male bees fly about looking for mates, *Ophrys sphegodes* offers what appears to be a suitable target and the duped males eagerly engage the flower in copulation (more precisely, this action is termed pseudocopulation). While this process offers no benefit to the bee or the propagation of his species, his vigorous efforts ensure pollination of the flowers.

The dull brown, blotchy tones and musty fragrance of some Bulbophyllums can successfully mimic a type of fungus that is preferred by a species of fly as a home for its eggs and a subsequent food source for the emerging maggots. Fooled by the imitation fungus the flies lay their eggs and, in the process, touch the reproductive parts of the flower, thereby assisting in pollination. Many species of *Cirrhopetalum* attract carrion-feeding insects, such as flies, with a pungent fragrance of rotting meat which is complemented by flowers that have the form and colour of rotting flesh.

CARING FOR ORCHIDS

As you consider the type, colour, size and fragrance of the orchids you would like to have in your home, take some time to do a brief analysis of the growing conditions your environment offers. Orchids grow best in climates that approximate their natural habitat. So, for instance, if you live in the tropics, with no air conditioning in your home, it will be tricky to grow an orchid that enjoys a cooler climate, such as an Odontoglossum. Extraordinary efforts may keep the plant alive, but it will not thrive. It is better to be practical and enjoy success with an orchid suited to your local climate and home environment. When making a decision, the main factors you need to evaluate are temperature, light, ventilation, heating and humidity.

BUYING ORCHIDS

Orchids are widely available from retail plant outlets, garden centres and even supermarkets, as well as from specialist nurseries and at orchid society meetings and shows. Each has its advantages and disadvantages and at least one of these options is sure to be available in your area. Where you choose to buy may depend on what you are looking for.

Popular orchids come from commercially tested stock that has long-lasting properties and is resistant to most pests and diseases. Commercial growers can cultivate the plants easily and mass produce them in large enough quantities to sell at an affordable price. Affordability is the main advantage to purchasing from a non-specialist outlet.

When you are buying a plant from a general retailer, inspect it closely to ensure that it is healthy and blemish free. Ask if the plant has recently come into the store (t may have arrived in good condition but been improperly handled throughout its shelf-life). Glean as much information as you can from the sales assistant, but bear in mind that you may not get much, if any,

An orchid auction in progress in Nagoya, Japan.

Yamamoto-type Dendrobiums on sale at an auction in Aalsmeer, The Netherlands.

specific orchid information. Garden centres may have a specialist who visits on a particular day to offer advice, or give demonstrations on potting or dividing.

Orchids at general retail outlets will most likely have a tag identifying the type of plant, but no specific name, and you will have to do some independent research for more information. There is no problem with buying an 'unnamed' orchid unless you intend to enter it in a competition.

Almost any type of orchid is available from the thousands of vendors advertising on the Internet. This is not a recommended option for new buyers, and even experienced buyers need to be cautious about selecting a reputable source. The Internet is a very useful source of information, however, and a few popular sites are listed on page 155.

SPECIALIST ORCHID NURSERIES

These are the best option if you are fortunate enough to have one in your area. Here, you will find a wide selection and can be confident that the plants have been properly maintained. You should benefit from the assistance of experienced staff. Most nurseries also offer free telephone advice. The plants will be tagged with their specific names – a requirement if you intend to exhibit (see page 64).

Repotting services may be offered for a small fee. Many specialist nurseries give demonstrations or hold classes on basic orchid care. Some go one step further, with full-day courses that cover orchid cultivation and care in more detail.

ORCHID SHOWS

Local orchid groups or societies have a wealth of experienced growers willing to share their knowledge and assist potential growers and society members. Many hold annual shows where you will find a wide range of named plants, as well as orchid care and maintenance equipment, books, videos and other information. The plant vendors at these shows normally have stock suited to the local environment and can offer advice on growing appropriate plants.

Mass production of *Epidendrum* orchids for the retail market has helped to increase their popularity, but it has become a large-scale business, as at this commercial nursery in Japan.

CHOOSING AN ORCHID

Wherever you decide to purchase your orchid, a few simple guidelines will help you to make the right decision. The plant should be clean, unblemished and free of any pests or fungus. If you are buying an orchid for the first time it is best to buy a mature plant in flower with a few unopened buds. Young plants require precise care and until you are familiar with the maintenance requirements you stand a greater chance of success with a mature plant. In addition, an orchid in flower reveals colour and possibly fragrance that can be immediately enjoyed and as the buds open you will be able to get a good sense of the flower's life cycle.

If you are buying an orchid to add to an existing collection, remember to isolate the plant for two weeks to be sure it is free of pests or disease. Insect infestations and infections can easily and quickly spread to other plants. If, during the isolation period, you notice that the new plant is infected, return it to the vendor and request a replacement or a refund.

DEVELOPING ORCHIDS FOR THE MARKET

Mass production of orchids as a worldwide industry began in the 1960s with the development of tissue culture cultivation, a technique whereby a minute piece of tissue is taken from the mother plant and divided again and again, producing numerous identical plants, or mericlones. This method is economical, faster than reproduction by division (see page 57), and allows commercial growers to offer affordable, high-quality plants. While tissue culture cultivation has accelerated the pace of plant production, market demand has challenged growers to offer a wider variety of plants.

It can take six to eight years from laboratory to marketplace, which makes plant development challenging. Several hundred seedlings are grown. From among these, just a few plants meet a list of very strict criteria and are chosen for production. The parent plant is selected and tested in the greenhouse before tissue is taken from it and cultivated in the laboratory.

Plant selectors look at the colour and quality of the flowers, the number of flowers on a stem, the number of stems on a mature plant and, in the case of cut flower varieties, for strong stems. If the plant is intended for sale as a pot plant, it should have flowers placed well above the foliage, which must be clean and in proportion to a specified height-width ratio. The plant must also have good disease-resistant properties. Only if all these criteria have been met does mass production begin.

ESTABLISHING A COLLECTION

Once the bug has bitten it can be very tempting to buy every pretty orchid you see, but you must be resolute. Establishing a worthwhile collection requires some planning and strategy. A good collection has focus and direction, reflecting the interests and skills of the grower.

Firstly, appreciate and understand your time limits, budget, space and the conditions that you are able to offer. Budget for the best possible plants, even if healthy, well-established specimens from recommended nurseries cost a little more. The first few years can prove to be expensive, as you may be overly enthusiastic in buying and lose some plants to inexperience.

Some collectors choose to specialize in a single genus and build a collection to include some stud plants that can be crossed and cultivated. There is a great thrill in seeing your seedlings flower after tending the plants from infancy. You may also be able to sell selected seedlings through your local orchid society. Not only would this assist in supporting your hobby, it would also help the society that, most likely, depends on a percentage of takings to boost their funds.

Serious collectors should visit specialized growers who offer selected seedlings and divisions of superior and awarded orchids. Apart from the pleasure and challenge of growing such a plant, if you wish to exhibit, it is important to be able to show something different from everyone else.

Orchid nurseries that breed their own hybrids often have one-of-a-kind seedlings. They may even import good quality plants from foreign breeders to complement their own stock. These nurseries usually stock a range of sundry items for growers, and can offer professional advice to help you build your collection.

The mixed private collection for a keen hobbyist in a well-maintained greenhouse.

Cultivated orchids grow here in optimal conditions of moisture and humidity thanks to constant spraying of water from overhead or under-bench sprinklers. The flow of water can be regulated in accordance with the external air temperature.

CREATING THE CORRECT GROWING ENVIRONMENT INDOORS

Temperature, humidity, ventilation and light all play a role in determining which orchids will grow and thrive in a particular environment. Whether your plants are grown outdoors, in an environmentally controlled greenhouse or hothouse, or in your front room, they will do better if the circumstances suit them.

TEMPERATURE

Temperature requirements vary widely even among the different orchid species, but generally, they may be divided into three main groups based on their preferred climates. The basic temperature groupings below reflect lowest night-time temperature the plant will tolerate for prolonged periods. At maximum levels, most orchids will become stressed if they are exposed to sustained high temperatures.

Cool-climate orchids (see pages 78–101)

Cool-climate orchids come from cool mountainous regions where the average temperature is chilly, even in summer. They grow best in daytime temperatures of between 18° and 27°C (65–80°F) with night-time temperatures of between 8° and 16°C (52–60°F).

Orchids for intermediate climates (see pages 102–123)

These orchids come from similar conditions, but grow at lower altitudes that experience slightly warmer temperatures. Suitable daytime temperatures range between 20° and 24°C (68–75°F) with night-time temperatures ranging between 13° and 16°C (58–60°F)

Warm-climate orchids (see pages 124–147)

Orchids from tropical and subtropical zones are used to a temperature that is consistently warm all year round with only minor fluctuations between day- and night-time temperatures. These species require a more constant daytime temperature of between 24° and 27°C (75–80°F) and overnight temperatures of 18–20°C (65–68°F).

Orchids are quite amenable to some moderate temperature fluctuations; indeed, they play a part in the life cycle of these plants: cool nights, warm days and seasonal fluctuations within an appropriate range signal their vital rest and growth cycles. It is very important to monitor minimum and maximum temperatures, however, as prolonged exposure to extremes will inhibit healthy growth and possibly kill the plant.

Additional humidity can be made available with the use of wet pads, fans, spray systems and humidifiers. Ensure that the fan you invest in is strong enough to cope with prolonged daily use.

You may be tempted to create artificial conditions within your home (such as air-conditioning in summer or heating in winter) to grow a type of orchid that is naturally unsuited to your climate. While this is not impossible, it could prove costly and even disappointing. There are a number of climate-specific orchids on the market and you are sure to get more pleasure from growing one that will thrive in your home environment.

Orchids require brief, but regular maintenance in the form of watering, misting and examining for signs of pest infestation or disease, so position the plant in a visible spot where you can enjoy its beauty and be reminded to care for it regularly.

LIGHT

Most orchids, particularly the more popular species, come from environments where the sunlight can be intense at tree canopy level, but is filtered by thick plant growth lower down the trunk. With this in mind, think about your chosen type of orchid and where you want to position the plant in relation to the windows in your home and the seasonal direction and intensity of sunlight. Most orchids require several hours of sunlight a day, but you may have to experiment to create the correct quality and intensity of light to suit your plant.

A few orchids, like cattleyas, laelias and vandas, can tolerate strong direct sun, but most prefer filtered light. This is easily achieved with blinds or curtains, or you can simply move the plant further into the room, away from direct light. If more light is required, you can mount a fluorescent light fixture on the window frame to augment the natural light. If your home lighting is thoroughly inadequate, special grow lights are available at general nurseries or you can devise your own light, using cool-white fluorescent tubes hung directly above the plants.

VENTILATION

Good ventilation will help your orchids flourish, but be careful of placing the plant in direct line of cold draughts; either window draughts in winter or air conditioning draughts in summer. When the weather is right, a fresh breeze from an open window is best, but even a small oscillating fan will keep an indoor atmosphere buoyant. The idea is to keep the indoor air lively, as orchids do not grow well in a stale, still environment.

This orchid, planted in a landscaped garden, is happily climbing up the trunk of a palm tree.

HUMIDITY

Orchids crave humidity. If you live in a region that has cold winters, be aware that central heating rapidly depletes moisture from the air. In these circumstances, a small humidifier placed in the growing area will help maintain constant humidity. Bathrooms may offer a nice, humid spot. In a very hot, dry atmosphere, orchids can be misted frequently and fairly inexpensively. For large collections, wet-pad evaporative coolers can be installed.

MOVING ORCHIDS OUTDOORS

In temperate climates, once the threat of frost or extremely cold temperatures has passed, many orchids enjoy spending spring and summer outdoors in the fresh air. Requirements for orchids grown outdoors are much the same as those for indoor plants: temperature, light, ventilation and humidity.

TEMPERATURE

In some parts of the world, it is not uncommon to experience sudden and dramatic midsummer heatwaves. Orchids don't like scorching heat, so be prepared to move your plant to a cooler location and provide plenty of humidity. On particularly cold spring evenings, your plant may have to be moved to a more sheltered or enclosed area to protect it.

LIGHT

Pay attention to seasonal changes in the sun's movement. Full midday sun is far too intense for most plants, so try to find a shady location with gentle early morning or late afternoon light.

VENTILATION

While orchids enjoy free-flowing, gentle summer breezes, try to position potted plants in an area that is sheltered from stronger gusts of wind so that they don't get toppled over.

HUMIDITY

Plants dry out more quickly in the summer heat and require more frequent watering. They also require at least as much, if not more, misting outdoors than they do indoors.

CARE AND MAINTENANCE OVERVIEW

Orchids are not as difficult to care for and maintain as many people think. If you follow some simple guidelines, with continuity and persistance, your orchids will give you months, and even years, of pleasure.

WATERING

Water requirements vary according to temperature, seasonal conditions and the growth cycle of the plant. Orchids take up more water during their active growing season when they are expending additional energy to support new growth. A few guidelines will help you determine the correct watering routine.

❀ Keep the plant moist, but not soggy. With experience, you can check the moisture level by judging the weight of the pot.

❀ Under average conditions, plants need watering once or twice a week.

❀ If in doubt, mist the plant rather than water it, and err on the side of under-watering, as there is nothing that will kill a plant faster than drowning its roots in a water-logged pot. Misting provides enough moisture and keeps the leaves free of dust and unwanted pests.

❀ Take the plant to a sink and water it from the top, allowing the water to run completely through the potting medium in order to flush out salts and excessive mineral deposits or accumulations. This is also a good time to mist the plant.

❀ If a plant has been neglected and has become exceedingly dry, keep misting it on a regular basis, but don't over-water it.

Orchids can easily be cultivated indoors. When watering is necessary, stand the plants on the kitchen draining board and water them from the top, leave to stand for a while and then return them to their place.

❀ Be sensitive to seasonal changes, such as very hot summer temperatures, which will accelerate water evaporation.

❀ Central heating creates a very dry environment, so you may need to water indoor plants more frequently in winter.

Regular misting is necessary to avoid dehydration, particularly in warm climates or in centrally heated rooms. When necessary, foliar fertilizer can be added to the water, but take care not to exceed the recommended dosage.

MISTING

All orchids enjoy a daily morning misting, using a fine, light spray to moisten the leaves. Mist plants in the morning to allow the water to evaporate throughout the warmth of the day. Water evaporates more slowly in cool night-time temperatures, and excess moisture can damage or cause bacterial rot.

HUMIDITY

Maintain humidity around the plant by placing the pot on a tray of wet pebbles or clay pellets. These should be kept damp, but the pot should not rest in a pool of water.

LIGHT

Provide a minimum of six hours per day of filtered light. Orchids will tolerate inadequate light, but may not produce flowers. Leaf colour will tell you if you've got the lighting right. Orchid leaves should be pale to medium green. If they begin to turn very dark green, it's an indication that the plant needs more light or that it is being overfed with nitrogen. If they begin to bleach out and turn pale, the plant is getting too much light and should be relocated to prevent scorching.

FEEDING

Although many orchids are light feeders, some nutrients are required to keep them in good health, particularly during the growing period, so feed lightly but regularly. Experienced growers sometimes mix a combination of nutrients specifically for a particular plant, but simple, low-maintenance feeding schemes work well for most orchids. Feed once a week with a good quality 30-10-10 nitrogenous fertilizer (diluted to half the recommended dosage in spring). Throughout summer, use a general-purpose feed (e.g. 18-18-18 or similar ratio fertilizer). A formula that is high in potash (10-30-20), diluted to half the recommended strength, can be used as a bloom booster, as it contains more potassium and less nitrogen, a combination that encourages flowering. If you fertilize regularly, use weaker solutions of any appropriate fertilizer.

Morning	Check all your orchids and provide them with water if necessary.
Mid-morning	Spray greenhouse floors.
Midday	Mist the plants if necessary (specifically on extremely hot days).
Mid-afternoon	Mist again.
Late afternoon	Check all of your plants to ensure that there is no water left on any one of the leaves from earlier waterings.
Weekly	Fertilize as necessary. Check for any pests and treat (see pages 38–43). Stake any emerging flower stems.

Keep walkways clean and free from plant debris which can attract unwanted pests and diseases.

MAINTAINING A HEALTHY ENVIRONMENT

Cleanliness is particularly important in a greenhouse, where humidity encourages the growth of algae and moss, which attract a variety of unwelcome insects, slugs and snails. A spotlessly clean environment will discourage pests as well as limit diseases, so keep the plant free from weeds, slime and dust, and remove fading flowers and dead leaves promptly so that the potting medium contains no rotting debris.

Make sure your plants get plenty of fresh, lively ventilation, as bacterial spores thrive in stale, damp air. Keep some space between the plants to allow for the free flow of air all around them. While grouping plants will help to maintain humidity, over-crowding inhibits buoyant air movement and makes it easier for pests or diseases to pass from one plant to another.

Water early in the day to give the plants a chance to dry off before the cool night temperatures set in. Leaving plants wet overnight makes them vulnerable to the bacterial and fungal diseases created by cold, damp conditions. Some diseases are easily spread by water, so prevent splashes when watering and never water one plant with the runoff from another.

Keeping tools and pots clean

Use clean tools when repotting, dividing plants, removing old leaves, or cutting flower stems. After use clean the tools thoroughly or sterilize in a flame before using again to avoid transferring any disease, virus or infection from one plant to another. To clean tools, use rubbing alcohol – usually 70 per cent denatured ethyl alcohol (methylated spirits), a 50:50 solution of household bleach and water, or any proprietary sterilizing solution.

Dirty hands can spread disease. Disposable plastic or latex gloves come in handy when repotting or dividing more than one plant. Otherwise, wash your hands thoroughly with a disinfectant soap between handling plants. Mealy bug, for example, is easily spread.

It is advisable to use new pots, but if you are going to reuse old ones, they must be cleaned and disinfected. Dispose of old compost (never reuse it) and use a brush to scrub out any remaining particles. Soak pots for at least 30 minutes in a solution of one part bleach to 15 parts water. Plastic pots can simply be rinsed and dried, but clay pots will absorb the bleach solution and should be soaked in clean, fresh water for another 30 minutes and then allowed to dry thoroughly before use.

PESTS AND DISEASES

Whether an orchid collection is grown outdoors, in pots in your home, or in a climatically controlled greenhouse you will eventually be faced with the problem of pests and diseases. These unwelcome visitors spoil the appearance of plants by marking or disfiguring the leaves or impairing new growth. It is always disappointing to find that the long-awaited buds of a cherished orchid have been chewed by a foraging slug, or the pollen removed by a hungry mouse. Orchids suffer from much the same infestations of pests as most other plants and should be treated in a similar manner. Successfully controlling pests and diseases often lies in prevention rather than cure, so regularly check your plants for signs of pests, viruses or diseases.

As a first step, purchase your orchids from a reputable nursery; carefully grown plants are usually resistant to fungal or bacterial diseases and more likely to be free of pests. If possible, house newly purchased plants in a quarantine area, or at least away from your existing collection, until you are confident that the new plants are pest- and disease-free.

TIPS FOR USING INSECTICIDES

✿ Select the correct insecticide or pesticide for the job.

✿ Always read the manufacturer's instructions and be sure to mix and apply products precisely according to directions.

✿ Apply in moderate temperatures to avoid damaging the plant.

✿ Keep pets and children away from the area when spraying.

✿ Protect yourself with gloves, a face mask and goggles when spraying.

✿ Thoroughly wash any part of your skin that comes into contact with the solution.

✿ Safely dispose of any unused mixture.

✿ Store insecticides out of reach of children, preferably under lock and key.

Aphids are attracted to many different varieties of plant, including orchids.

Here mealy bugs, also known as wooly aphids, are attacking emerging new growth.

There is nothing worse than entering the greenhouse only to discover that a prize bloom has been destroyed by snails and slugs during the night.

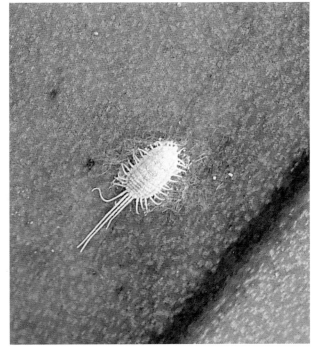

A mature mealy bug on the underside of a *Phalaenopsis* leaf.

COMMON PESTS

Pests	Description	Treatment
Ants	Small red or black ants feed on the honeydew that is secreted by aphids. Ants transport scale from one plant to another, thus rapidly spreading scale infestations. Ants also establish nests in pots; these break down the compost and prevent proper root aeration.	Treat the entire plant with an appropriate insecticide.
Aphids	Very small, but visible green, black, brown or orange insects that suck the sap from new plant growth. They multiply rapidly in warm, dry weather and secrete a substance called honeydew that attracts ants. Honeydew on leaves also causes sooty mould.	For minor infestations, spray aphids with a jet of tepid water or wash the infected area by immersing it in a solution of insecticidal soap and water. Aphids may also be removed by hand, or wiped off with a damp cotton swab. For serious infestations, use a general insecticide. Check frequently for these persistant pests.
False spider mite	Even smaller than red spider mites, these are evidenced by silvery coloured pitting on the top and undersides of leaves.	Treat as for red spider mites (see opposite).
Leaf hopper	Tiny, white, sap-sucking flies found on the underside of leaves, on flowers, and particularly on new growth	Hang up sticky fly-traps or treat the plant with an appropriate insecticide.
Leaf miner	Small grubs known for spreading virus-related diseases that destroy leaves and stems.	Cut away damaged stems and leaves and apply systemic insecticide.
Mealy bugs	A common orchid pest, these oval, fluffy grey-white insects with filaments projecting from their bodies are sucking insects often found on the underside of leaves, leaf axils and new growth, and will also attack flowers. They secrete honeydew, which causes sooty mould on leaves.	For minor infestations, use a cotton swab and clean the infested area with water and a mild liquid detergent or insecticidal soap to remove adults. They are persistent pests that may take months to eradicate. If flowers are badly infested, cut off the blooms.
Rats and mice	Rodents are attracted to the warm greenhouse environment and enjoy eating flower pollen. They cause damage by scampering up stems to reach the pollen, and shorten the flower's life.	Use commercial poison or set traps.

COMMON PESTS

Pests	Description	Treatment
Red spider mite	This common orchid pest, particularly prevalent in soft-leafed plants such as *Cymbidiums* or *Lycastes*, is barely visible to the naked eye, but clearly evidenced by a web-like film on the underside of leaves. Sap sucking insects, red spider mites destroy leaf cells, causing yellowing and irreparable damage to the leaf surface.	Regular misting on the top and underside of leaves can help prevent infestations. Clean affected leaves with insecticidal soap and water to kill the adult mites. Repeat every 10 days to kill any eggs. Alternatively, use a recommended miticide.
Scale insects	There are several varieties. Leaves frequently appear to be covered in a round or oval-shaped brown or tan shell (scale). Mobile when young, the adults rest on the under-side of leaves or beneath the leaf sheath, singly or in colonies. These sap-sucking insects leave yellow patches on leaves; they also secrete honeydew which causes sooty mould and attracts ants. Very persistant pests.	Use a soft brush and insecticidal soap and water to remove, being careful not to damage the leaf. Alternatively clean leaves using a cotton swab dipped in a 50:50 solution of water and denatured alcohol. Serious infestations require several applications of systemic insecticide.
Snails and slugs	These common greenhouse pests favour seedlings and soft foliage plants, eating through root tips, flower buds and pseudobulbs. Most active after dark, their movements are evidenced by tracks of silvery slime.	Vigilance is the best defence against these nocturnal pests that crawl in through vents and small crevices. Organic control methods usually involve luring them to feed in a saucer of beer or under a lettuce leaf, then collecting them by hand the next morning. Commercial slug and snail pellets are very effective, but harmful to curious domestic pets, so use them with caution.
Thrips	Tiny greyish, winged insects that settle on the underside of leaves. Chewing insects, they scrape the leaf surface for sap, causing scarring and discolouration.	Treat the plant with appropriate insecticide.
Weevils	These hard-bodied beetles, usually dull-coloured, chew into the soft tissue areas of the plant. The damage looks much like that of caterpillars.	Spray or dust the plant with the appropriate insecticide.

COMMON DISEASES

Diseases	Description	Treatment
Basal rot/ damping off	Fungal disease that withers the stem of young seedlings. May be caused by unclean pots or potting medium, overcrowding, or over-watering.	Apply fungicide to infected plants. Repot them and reduce watering, increase ventilation.
Bacterial brown spot	This appears as a brown, watery blister on the leaf and spreads very quickly. It will kill the plant if the infection reaches the crown. Thrives in cold, wet conditions and develops when leaves are allowed to remain wet. *Phalaenopsis* plants are most vulnerable.	Isolate the affected orchid and remove infected leaves with a sterilized cutting tool. Control by spraying with a bactericide according to the manufacturer's instructions. Move infected plants to a drier environment until the disease is controlled.
Brown rot	Begins as a small brown spot on the leaf that quickly enlarges. Infected plants give off a spicy odour. This disease will eventually kill the plant if it reaches the crown. *Paphiopedilums* are most vulnerable.	Treat as for bacterial brown spot. A good dusting of cinnamon powder usually helps.
Black rot	A fungal infection that may attack any part of the plant, including pseudobulbs, leaves or rhizomes. It is signalled by the infected area turning black and watery. Often caused by over-watering. *Cattleyas* are most vulnerable.	Remove parts of the plant that are infected. Spray with recommended fungicide according to pack instructions. Avoid over-watering.
Root rot	A fungal infection of the roots. Plants will show signs of declining health and infected roots will turn brown. Caused by over-watering and potting medium that is decayed or otherwise poorly aerated.	Use a sterilized cutting tool to remove all dead tissue. Repot in a clean pot with fresh growing medium and treat with a recommended fungicide according to the manufacturer's instructions. Avoid over-watering.
Leaf spotting	Unattractive but benign fungus that appears as small brown or black spots on leaves. All orchids are vulnerable.	Spray with recommended fungicide according to the instructions. Ensure that the growing conditions are optimal.

COMMON VIRUSES

Diseases	Description	Treatment
Sooty mould	A soft black fungal growth that forms on the honeydew deposited by aphids, mealy bugs and scale insects and reduces the amount of light reaching the leaves, causing the plant to deteriorate.	Wash leaves with soapy water, or use a 50:50 solution of water and denatured alcohol. Get rid of the insect pests that cause the problem (see aphids, page 40).
Cymbidium mosaic	The most common orchid virus, this appears as dark, sunken patches or streaks on leaves. Plants will continue to grow, but will lack vigour and can infect other plants.	There is no remedy. To prevent it spreading, you must destroy the affected plants.
Tobacco mosaic and yellow bean mosaic	Leaves will become mottled with irregular patches of green and yellow and flowers will show streaky, dark colouration. These viruses particularly affect *Cymbidiums* and *Masdevallias*.	Destroy the infected plant.
Odontoglossum ringspot virus	Round blemishes appear on the leaves in concentric circles, eventually affecting the flowers, which emerge deformed.	Destroy the infected plant.

PREVENTING DISEASE

- Check regularly for visible signs of pests and diseases.

- Maintain a clean and well-balanced growing environment.

- Buy only healthy plants.

- Quarantine all new plants for two weeks.

- Sterilize cutting tools and disinfect used pots with a bleach solution.

- Never reuse compost or water a plant with runoff from another plant.

Carefully staked and well cared for, this *Vanda* Robert's Delight is in perfect health. Ensure that your orchids look like this at all times to prevent costly losses.

USING INSECTICIDES

Before rushing to spray just any available insecticide on an infested plant, take a moment to ascertain the degree of the problem. While it is important to deal with any infestation promptly, first try practical, non-chemical solutions, then monitor the situation very closely and proceed accordingly.

Visible pests can be removed by hand, or wiped from the plant with soapy water, or with a cotton swab dipped in denatured alcohol. Environmentally friendly pest control products are widely available and may deal with the problem as effectively as chemical insecticides. Minor infestations of common pests can often be managed by introducing natural predators, such as using ladybirds to control aphids.

If an insecticide is the only solution to a pest infestation, it is important to take precautions when mixing and applying chemicals to avoid damaging the plant or harming yourself.

Get professional advice on which insecticide to use and how to use it and follow all the instructions carefully. The wrong product, or an incorrect dilution, can burn or even kill a plant. Repeated applications may be necessary to completely eradicate infestation, but be aware that overuse of insecticides and fungicides can cause irreparable damage and cause a condition called phytotoxicity (a toxic buildup within the plant).

Whenever possible, apply insecticides when the sky is overcast, or early in the morning before temperatures peak. Plants are easily stressed in high temperatures and are therefore more vulnerable to chemical damage. Try to choose a still day to prevent the spray or powder from blowing around the area rather than resting on the plant.

Protect yourself by wearing gloves, protective clothing, and a face mask or goggles to avoid inhalation or eye irritation. If any part of the body is exposed to chemicals or insecticides, wash it off as soon as possible. Of course, unused chemicals and insecticides must be stored in a properly locked cupboard out of the reach of children or anyone who does not know how to use them responsibly. Unused solution should be discarded.

DISEASES AND VIRUSES

Most orchid diseases come from prolonged exposure to improper growing conditions, such as excess cold, inadequate ventilation or over-watering. Sometimes, in spite of your best efforts to maintain a healthy growing environment, disease will strike. Plant diseases can be difficult to diagnose, but be on the lookout for problems and act swiftly to contain them.

Viruses are easily transmitted and can wipe out an entire collection if they are not dealt with swiftly and thoroughly. Some viruses are fatal. In such cases there is no option but to destroy the infected plant by burning it.

Thriving pots of *Epidendrum* orchids provide an attractive focal point in this well-kept garden.

PROVIDING A CONTROLLED ENVIRONMENT FOR YOUR ORCHIDS

As your collection grows you may consider housing your plants where the growing conditions can be precisely controlled. There are many different types of structure which constitute a greenhouse; the right option for you depends on your local climate, space, budget and available time. Also, think about whether you want to grow a selection of orchids or specialize in one genus, as these factors may influence your decision.

SUNROOM OR CONSERVATORY

An existing sunroom or conservatory can be easily and economically converted to an orchid-friendly environment with a few climate-control modifications.

Blinds allow you to regulate the amount of strong sunlight that is directed at the plants. If your plants are grouped in one part of the room, consider painting the glass roof above them to reduce direct overhead sun. If you plan to build a sunroom with your orchid collection in mind, try to position it where direct sunlight is minimal, particularly in summer. An adjacent tree or large bush may be exploited to provide a semi-shaded environment in at least part of the room.

Controlling light also helps to moderate excessive summer heat. A simple portable fan can provide ventilation and, if the climate permits, keeping the door open will provide a welcome breeze. If the room is not centrally heated in winter, a portable heater will help to maintain correct temperatures. On sunny winter days the room may be pleasantly warm, but a heater will most certainly be required at night. Humidity can be created by placing the plants on humidity trays and misting them regularly. An electric humidifier also helps to keep the environment moist.

In homes with a combination sun-and-poolroom, be aware that a swimming pool helps to create a humid environment for the plants, but chlorine gas can be extremely harmful.

In climates that experience extreme sunlight and high temperatures, shading material is stretched on suspended frames above the roof to create a cushion of air that will create a buffer from the intense heat.

SHADE HOUSE

Suitable for warmer climates, a shade house is the least expensive option. It is basically an enclosed structure made of wire mesh and shade cloth attached to poles staked in the ground. Some structures also have a shade cloth roof.

The shade house should be positioned where there is air movement, but sheltered from extreme wind. A location with partial sun makes it easier to control heat and maintain correct humidity. It should be in proximity to a tap, to make misting and watering easier, particularly if you decide to install an overhead misting system.

The plants can be placed on wooden benches (slatted tops are best as they allow for air circulation and water runoff. Special staging benches (wooden-frame benches with galvanized wire top), are available but will add to your expense. If the roof is sturdy enough, you can add hanging baskets.

LATH HOUSE

Common in subtropical and tropical climates, a lath house is a sturdier form of shade house, with walls constructed of wooden slats supported by staked poles.

Plants may be hung from the roof or the walls. The location considerations are the same as for a shade house.

Lath houses require quite a bit of attention, as humidity can fall easily when the wind blows; however, this can be overcome by installing a spraying system.

POLYTHENE TUNNEL

Polythene tunnels make effective orchid environments. They come in various sizes and forms, the most basic being polythene sheeting stretched over galvanized tubing. Tunnels are easily erected and reasonably inexpensive in general.

One disadvantage is that polythene may not last more than a few years before it starts to disintegrate from the effects of the sun. Shade cloth can be erected overhead to give additional protection.

Old or weathered plastic sheeting can easily tear in windy or stormy conditions. If possible, position your tunnel in a semi-sheltered spot, out of the path of strong winds. In mild conditions, you can open both end flaps of the tunnel, allowing the breeze to provide free ventilation.

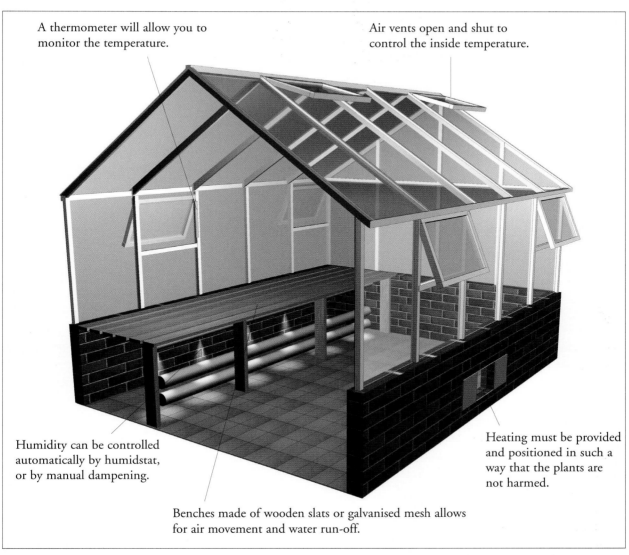

A thermometer will allow you to monitor the temperature.

Air vents open and shut to control the inside temperature.

Humidity can be controlled automatically by humidstat, or by manual dampening.

Heating must be provided and positioned in such a way that the plants are not harmed.

Benches made of wooden slats or galvanised mesh allows for air movement and water run-off.

A simple greenhouse structure, as illustrated here, does not have to be hugely expensive. If well maintained, the structure will last for many years.

THE GREENHOUSE

When fitted with the proper equipment, a greenhouse, or glasshouse as it is sometimes called, will provide optimal growing conditions for your plants all year long. Greenhouses come in a variety of shapes and sizes and can be purchased as DIY kit or custom-built structures. Prices range accordingly, but a greenhouse remains a costly affair no matter which way you look at it.

When positioning a greenhouse, choose a level piece of ground to make construction easier. If this is not possible, you must budget for ground clearing and levelling.

Avoid placing the structure directly under large trees, particularly deciduous ones, as seasonal fluctuations in sunlight created by the absence or presence of leaves will complicate your light and heat management and also makes the roof vulnerable to falling debris. At best, you will have the task of keeping the roof structure clean; at worst a large branch may fall and break the glass. However, some adjacent shelter will aid climate management by providing cooling shade to the surrounding area in summer and breaking up a cold, heavy wind in winter.

A minimum/maximum thermometer is essential in any greenhouse in order to monitor the internal temperature range and adjust it if need be.

As a rule, in the northern hemisphere a north/south position provides maximum light, while in the southern hemisphere structures are best positioned east/west.

Once you have established the greenhouse environment, it is relatively easy to maintain. For convenience, the greenhouse should be close to your home with easy access along a clear path. (You will appreciate this on a cold or rainy night when you set off to perform your final inspection). Building the structure in close proximity to your home will also simplify the installation of the electricity and water connections you need for heating, cooling and humidity control equipment.

STRUCTURE

There is no correct size for a greenhouse, except that it must be high enough so that you can comfortably stand in it and, ideally, suspend hanging baskets or plants above head height. Some greenhouses are designed to accommodate extensions that can be added as your collection grows. Bear in mind, however, that these increase length not width, so it is best to invest upfront in the largest structure your budget permits. Whether you have one professionally constructed or buy a DIY kit, there are certain factors to consider.

Wooden or aluminium frame

This choice is basically one of aesthetics. Wood retains heat better than aluminium, which can reduce winter heating costs. On the other hand, it must be regularly treated to prevent weathering and rot which, over the years, will require an investment of time as well as materials. Aluminium frames are lightweight, sturdy, corrosion-resistant and virtually maintenance-free, but considerably more expensive than wooden structures.

Glass or polycarbonate panels

Both materials have advantages. Glass is an excellent transmitter of solar heat and is less expensive than polycarbonate, but it is vulnerable to damage by falling debris, heavy to work with in DIY construction, and some form of insulation is required in winter and shading in summer.

Polycarbonate, on the other hand, is lightweight, virtually unbreakable and may be textured or tinted to diffuse light in varying degrees. It is available in single sheets, twin-wall or triple-wall design for heat retention. It can be used in conjunction with glass in specific areas of the greenhouse, for example to create permanently diffused lighting in one roof section, or extra insulation without loss of light.

Brick or concrete side walls

A structure designed with brick or concrete side walls built up to bench height will retain more heat than a glass or polycarbonate ground-to-roof structure. Vents can be built into the base below bench level, but remember that all vents must be rodent proof. Floor-level vents are particularly desirable as they allow fresh air into the greenhouse in areas that experience very cold winter climates.

CLIMATE CONTROL

It is essential to maintain the correct balance of light, heat and humidity throughout the day and across the

Wet cooling systems require an extractor fan to draw the warm air across a wall of cool running water and through the cell systems.

Today's modern commerical greenhouses are monitored by sensitive computer systems that adjust the internal conditions automatically.

seasons. Depending on your schedule, budget and inclination, this process may be manual or automated. Either way, you must regularly monitor and adjust climate conditions. One point to ponder – the smaller the greenhouse, the more difficult it is to maintain a constant climate, as small greenhouses heat up faster and cool down more quickly than larger ones.

Heating

In cold climates, insulation will help to reduce your winter heating bills. If your structure is ground-to-roof glass, the panels below the staging benches can be insulated with polystyrene sheets. For the panels above bench height and for the roof panels, you can create the effect of 'double glazing' by affixing plastic sheeting or polythene lining (bubble wrap) to the glass panel frames. Leaving a small gap of air between the glass and the plastic sheeting helps to retain both heat and humidity.

Polycarbonate panels can also be positioned over the glass to provide very effective insulation, but this is a more expensive option.

An electric heater with a built-in thermostat will help you to achieve precise temperatures. Check the accuracy of the heater's thermostat by taking regular readings with a minimum/maximum thermometer (a very good investment). A heater can be an expensive option, whereas if a greenhouse is situated near to the house, the main boiler can easily be modified and a branch installed to service the greenhouse. A timer, either built-in or attached separately, is an added convenience and a bit of insurance if you find yourself unable to get to the greenhouse to make manual adjustments.

Paraffin heaters are not recommended as they emit harmful fumes which are toxic and can cause long-term damage to orchids, even killing them.

Ventilation

Roof ventilation is essential to expel summer heat, except in a greenhouse where cooling equipment or wet walls are installed and fans expel any excessive heat. Side vents are helpful in creating a cross-current of air and, if the option is available, vents below bench level are desirable. Roof ventilation also allows for the exchange of hot air for the fresh, cooling breezes that are beneficial to all orchids.

A portable or built-in electric fan helps reduce heat in summer and keeps the temperature uniform around the greenhouse in winter, preventing a build-up of pockets of cold air. An extractor fan helps to reduce heat, but tends to extract precious humidity along with the warm air and you will have to mist more frequently. There should be at least one adjustable roof vent to prevent heat build up. Ideally, vents should be situated at opposite ends of the greenhouse to provide a cross-current of air. Ventilation below bench level is also desirable.

While it is important that you take every opportunity to provide the plants with fresh, buoyant air, they will not appreciate a blast of cold night air, so vents must be adjusted regularly according to temperature changes. If your budget permits, buy automated vents that operate on a timer or a sensor.

Light

All greenhouses need some form of shading to regulate light and heat. Shade cloth, made of loosely woven fibres, is available in densities ranging from 20–90 per cent and can be attached to the structure with grommets. Check with the supplier how much shade is

GREENHOUSE MAINTENANCE

Maintaining a greenhouse is time consuming, but once you establish the correct routine you will be rewarded by thriving, healthy plants.

Monitoring It is important to monitor the greenhouse regularly and make adjustments according to changes in light and temperature. Automated systems will save time, but are costly. Visit the greenhouse at least twice a day to ensure that all equipment is operating correctly.

Cleaning Clean the glass, both inside and outside, particularly around the frames, to avoid a dusty buildup where moss can grow and to which slugs and insects will be attracted. An overly damp environment can be a breeding ground for moss and algae, which attracts slugs, snails and other pests. If the structure has partial walls, these should be washed periodically. An annual lime-washing of the walls will discourage ants, termites, slugs and snails.

Sweep up any debris where insects may hide, clean slimy dirt from the floor, and keep the pathways clean and free of weeds and dead leaves. Be sure to maintain the area under the benches, particularly in winter when rodents tend to make this area their home. If you use a floor liner, rinse it periodically to prevent the build up of old compost which, in combination with leafy debris, attracts insects.

Shading is important for a greenhouse environment, as the orchids must be shielded from direct sunlight. In this commercial greenhouse, aluminium shade cloth has been used.

provided by the cloth, e.g. 40 per cent shade cloth does not always offer 40 per cent shade. Light and temperature changes seasonally – attach the cloth at double thickness if you want additional light filtering without more heat. Shade cloth can be fitted over the entire greenhouse, allowing approximately 15–20cm (6–8in) clearance above the exterior glass for a free flow of air. It also ensures that direct sunlight hits the cloth first. Shade cloth screens can easily be removed in the autumn to maximize winter light.

✿ **Aluminized shade cloth** is a more expensive, but highly effective option. It is made of aluminized fibres that deflect external radiation by day, but at night reflect internal radiation from the floor of the greenhouse, assisting in heat retention.

✿ **Chalk-based paint** shading is useful, particularly on roofs. It generally lasts no more than a season before it washes off or fades away, but by the time it has deteriorated, the seasonal sun will have shifted and it will no longer be required. Of course, you must clean it off and re-apply it the following year. It is an inexpensive, but labour-intensive light-management option.

✿ **Louvres and roller blinds** are expensive but effective, and are reasonably easy to raise and lower. As with automated vents, they can be fitted with sensors so they will open and close automatically with the fluctuations in temperature.

Humidity

A simple way to create and maintain humidity is to 'damp down' the greenhouse regularly. This involves wetting the bench tops between the plants and allowing the runoff to thoroughly soak the floor underneath, as well as the pathway. The idea is to keep the environment consistently damp. In summer you may need to damp down three or four times a day, in winter less frequently (possibly only once a day). Also, the larger the space, the more quickly moisture will evaporate and the more frequently you will need to damp down. The plants should be misted at this time as well.

A manual pump sprayer is adequate for a small collection. For a larger collection, you can save time and effort by installing automatic misters with sprayers above and below the staging benches. These can be set to operate on a timer, saving you effort. In a small greenhouse, a portable humidifier can be a very effective aid in maintaining a consistent level of humidity.

CULTIVATION

While many orchids have specific cultivation requirements, there are plenty, particularly the popular species, that are no more difficult to grow than other plants.

REPOTTING

Most novice collectors purchase orchids in pots, which the plants will outgrow after one or two years. Orchids like snug quarters so, although a plant may appear to be uncomfortably cramped, a somewhat 'underpotted' environment is ideal. However, if a plant shows signs of pushing itself up and out of the pot, or if an abundance of pseudobulbs covers the top of the compost, it is time to offer a bit more space.

In addition to giving more space, another reason for repotting is that organic compost materials, such as bark, break down over time and need to be replaced. Apart from the powdery look and sour smell of the old compost, the plant will alert you by wrapping its aerial roots around the rim of the pot, thereby avoiding contact with the rotted medium.

Bear in mind that the epiphytic types usually extend a few of their aerial roots well above the rim of the pot so, for these species, this is not a sign of being pot-bound.

The best time to repot is in spring, when flowering is complete and a new growth cycle is beginning.

Pot size

Choose a pot just big enough to accommodate one or two year's growth. A pot that is about 5cm (2in) larger than the previous one should do. Orchids enjoy being snug, but also prefer to dry out a bit in between waterings. An excessively large pot of compost will retain more moisture than the roots can easily take up before they begin to drown or rot.

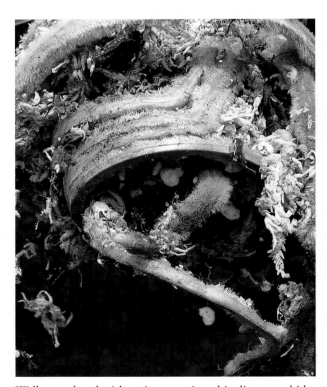

Well rooted and with active root tips, this slipper orchid is ready for the next size pot. Orchids enjoy being root-bound and should only be potted on into the same or a slightly larger sized pot.

REPOTTING AN ODONTOGLOSSUM

1 Remove the plant by gently coaxing its roots from the sides of the pot and sliding it out. A heavily pot-bound plant may not slide out very easily. If the pot is plastic, you can cut it away. A clay pot may have to be smashed to remove the plant.

2 If the root ball is in good condition, then simply place the plant into a bigger pot. If there is any rot at the roots, trim the root ball before repotting the plant into its new pot. Remove dead leaves and tidy the plant.

3 If the plant has outgrown the pot, examine the back bulbs. Brown, shrivelled, leafless back bulbs are dead and can be cut from the rhizome. Plump, green bulbs, even if leafless, are still active and should be left in place.

4 Place a layer of drainage material in the bottom of the new pot, adding enough compost so that the base of the plant will be level with the bottom of the pot rim. Polystyrene is a good deterrent for slugs and snails; broken pots or stones add weight to plastic pots.

5 Position the plant with the existing pseudobulbs towards one side of the pot, allowing space on the other side for new growth. Add more compost, pressing it down gently between the roots to secure the plant in the dampened compost.

6 For the next two weeks keep the plant in a semi-shaded, humid spot, but refrain from overwatering or feeding it. After this rest period, return the plant to its regular spot in the greenhouse and provide water and food regularly.

'POTTING ON' A YOUNG PLANT

Younger plants need to be moved into larger pots more frequently than mature plants in order to accommodate their accelerated growth. 'Potting on' does not involve any cutting or clean-up, it simply means moving the plant into a pot one size up and adding a bit more compost without disturbing the rapidly developing root ball.

1 Remove the plant from its pot. A young plant will slide out of its pot with just a few sharp taps.

2 The new pot should be 2.5cm (1in) larger in the case of this Cymbidium. Put clean drainage material into the pot and add a bit of fresh compost.

3 Position the plant so that new growth is level with the rim of the pot. Add more compost, pressing it down firmly into the crevices, being careful not to damage new root growth.

4 The plant should sit snugly in the potting medium to avoid any movement that would damage the fragile new roots.

CHOOSING THE CORRECT COMPOST

Ordinary compost mixes are not suitable for orchids. There are several specially formulated orchid composts that provide an adequate and reliable growing medium. You may want to add elements to cater for the needs of a specific plant or, if you have some experience in mixing compost, formulate your own. The correct potting mix depends upon the requirements of the plant. As a rule, orchids prefer a mix that is light and airy, absorbent but free draining, with a slightly acidic pH balance. A wide variety of organic and inorganic media can be used, either alone or in combination.

ORGANIC MEDIA

Peat	This growing medium is airy, retains moisture and works very well in combination with other media. Peat must be neutralized by adding dolomitic lime.
Bark chips	Bark chips may be coarsely or finely shredded for use in a potting mix for seedlings or mature plants. The chips retain moisture, but allow for a free flow of water.
Coconut fibre/ osmunda	Both coconut fibre and osmunda (fern fibre) help to keep the plant stable in the pot while allowing a free flow of water and air through the pot.
Sphagnum moss	Lightweight and porous, this good, moisture-retaining substance may be used in a mix and is sometimes used on its own as a medium.
Charcoal	Specially formulated for horticultural use, charcoal keeps the potting mix fresh and prevents souring. It is not ideal for use over long periods, however, as it does retain mineral salts.

INORGANIC MEDIA

Perlite	A white mineral substance used to provide aeration in a mix.
Pumice	Pumice is volcanic in origin and works well combined with osmunda or sphagnum.
Limestone gravel	This provides aeration and allows for a free flow of water.
Polystyrene balls	Used in the base of a pot, these provide aeration and allow for the free flow of water.
Rockwool	Made of glass fibres, it retains moisture while providing air pockets. It is effective, but hazardous: avoid skin contact and inhalation. Best when combined with foam.
Horticultural foam	A synthetic material with properties similar to rockwool, but without the health hazards. It can be used to aerate rockwool mixes.

This Cymbidium orchid is straining against the confines of its pot and urgently needs dividing and repotting.

PROPAGATION

Orchids are easily propagated by a variety of methods. Asexual, or vegetative, propagation (dividing a plant into smaller segments, or rooting a stem cutting), is the simplest technique, producing multiple identical plants.

Sexual propagation by seed, even among orchids in the wild, is a process fraught with uncertainty, as orchid seed requires very specific conditions to germinate naturally. However, scientific advancements over the years have made seed propagation an accessible and reliable method of reproduction, even for the home grower. As with any organism produced by sexual reproduction, each plant is genetically similar, but has unique characteristics.

Tissue culture propagation, which is primarily practiced on a commercial level, is a vegetative process whereby a slice of tissue is taken from an exceptionally fine parent plant and used to produce masses of genetically identical plants under sterile laboratory conditions.

VEGETATIVE PROPAGATION – DIVISION AND CUTTINGS

When a plant becomes unmanageably large, it is time to repot. This is also an excellent opportunity to multiply your orchid collection. Cymbidiums, for example, can be quite aggressive growers and are very easily divided.

HINTS ON DIVIDING AND CUTTING

- ✿ Use clean, sterilized cutting tools
- ✿ Apply sulphur powder to all cuts
- ✿ Wash hands thoroughly or wear rubber gloves when working with plants
- ✿ Always use clean, disinfected pots
- ✿ Pot with fresh compost

DIVIDING A CYMBIDIUM PLANT

1 Remove the plant from the pot. It may fall into segments, making it clear where divisions can be made. Using a sharp, sterilized blade, cut between the rhizomes and through the root ball.

2 Each division should have emerging new growths, at least three mature pseudobulbs, and a few back bulbs. Back bulbs are essential, because if the newly divided plant gets stressed before becoming established, it may need to call on the back bulb resources to survive.

3 Dust the cuts with sulphur powder to prevent rot. When potting up a new division, make sure that the plant is secured lightly but firmly to a stake, particularly if it has few viable roots. Any movement will damage emerging soft roots and will set the plant back.

ROOTING BACK BULBS

When dividing large plants you may have to cut off a few back bulbs. If these are very brown and shrivelled they are probably depleted of all resources and can be discarded but brown back bulbs that still feel plump and show signs of life can be coaxed into rooting. Bear in mind though that propagating from back bulbs can be a slow process, and it may take a few years for the new plants to become fully established.

Sympodial orchids like Cymbidiums and Lycastes respond well to this method; it is generally less successful with Odontoglossums and Oncidiums.

Although you can root back bulbs by placing them in trays filled with washed river sand or moss and keeping them damp, the plastic bag method is more reliable.

1 Wash the back bulb, place it in a plastic bag, tie a knot at the top and hang the bag from a hook under the growing bench, or in a cool, shaded area.

2 Check the bag regularly, as the bulb may begin to rot if it was badly damaged by the cut. More often than not, new growth will appear. When roots begin to emerge from the bulb, pot it up in your selected medium. Use the smallest possible pot so as to ensure just one year's growth.

Cymbidium back bulbs beginning to grow in a plastic bag.

TAKING STEM (CANE) CUTTINGS

Orchids such as *nobile*-type Dendrobiums and *Phaius tankervilleae* are easily propagated by rooting their stems.

1 Cut older, leafless stems just above the node. Cut the long stem into smaller sections, leaving at least two nodes per section.

2 Lay stem sections in a tray of moist river sand. Water and feed as you would a mature plant. Plantlets will sprout from the stems within six to eight weeks.

3 When the plantlets develop roots, pot them up. The plants will take several years to mature and will be identical to the parent plant. Treat the young plants as seedlings.

Dendrobium Oriental Smile 'Fantasy' AD/AOS, rewards the grower with a perfect flower on a plant grown from a *keiki*.

REMOVING A *KEIKI*

The adventitious growths, or offshoots, produced on the older canes of Dendrobium and a few other orchids, such as Oncidium and Phalaenopsis, are called *keiki*, a Hawaiian term that means 'little child'.

Dendrobiums produce *keikis* quite readily. As soon as they are big enough, the new plantlets can be removed from the mother plant, potted up and treated as young seedlings. Shown here is a specimen plant with *keikis*.

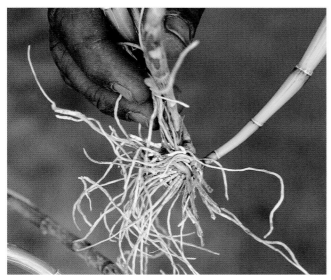

1 The *keikis* are easily removed from the main plant when they have developed a few strong roots.

2 This *keiki* has been potted on into its own basket and is thriving after only six months.

The parent plants: *Paph. rothschildianum* (left) and *Paph. micranthum* (right).

The progeny: *Paph.* Gloria Naugle (*rothschildianum* x *micranthum*).

SEED PROPAGATION

Propagating orchids from seed is more complicated and requires more patience than vegetative propagation, but it is exciting to breed selected orchids and follow the development of their progeny from seed to mature plant.

SELECTING THE PARENT PLANTS

When selecting plants for breeding it is important to research their backgrounds and determine if they are actually suitable mates. Choose parents that are healthy, strong growing plants, exhibiting good form and exceptional characteristics. Research the lineage of both parents as, if they come from a line of good strong hybrids they are more likely to produce good progeny.

If necessary, check the chromosomal compatibility of both plants. Professional breeders can determine the number of chromosomes by examining root tip samples under a microscope. Information on the chromosome count may be printed on the labels of plants for sale, or be supplied in the vendor's catalogue.

If you don't know the chromosome count of your prospective parent plants, just work with two related plants and you will stand a good chance of making a successful cross.

POLLINATING PLANTS

Pollinating plants is a very simple, but delicate process. After selecting the parent plants, remove the cap of both plants. Remove the pollinia of the mother plant so that it cannot be fertilized with its own pollen. Only when the pollinia has been removed from the mother plant, should you remove the pollen from the prospective father plant and place it on the receptive stigmatic surface of the mother plant.

After a successful pollination, the column will begin to swell as the pollen grains move towards the ovary, and the flower will wilt and fall off. The ovary will begin to swell and develop into a seed capsule. (If pollination was unsuccessful, the ovary will simply shrivel and die.) Depending on the type of orchid, it may take anywhere from three to 12 months for the ovary to become a fully ripened pod. When the pod turns yellow, the seed is ready for harvesting.

HARVESTING AND SOWING SEED

Orchid seed must be kept sterile, so it is important to harvest it before the pod splits open. Once harvested, sow the seed as soon as possible. Although it can be kept in cold storage, its viability reduces with age. Break the pod open into a small packet to avoid losing any of the minute seeds. Then simply scatter the seeds around the base of an established plant that will act as a 'mother plant'. Sown in close proximity to a mature plant, the seeds stand a chance of germinating with support from the mother plant's *mycorrhiza* and after several months you just may see a few plantlets forming.

Sowing seed around a mother plant is easy but a bit of a hit-and-miss affair. For guaranteed results send the seed to a specialist nursery or laboratory that offers a sowing service. Germinated in optimum conditions under professional guidance, the seeds will develop into plantlets within a few months. Alternatively, you can sow the seed at home using a method known as 'flasking'.

CHROMOSOME COUNTS: READING A PLANT LABEL

❀ Diploids have two sets of chromosomes. These are generally easy-growing, free-flowering plants. Most species are diploid, indicated by the symbol '2n'.

❀ Triploids, with three sets of chromosomes, are the product of breeding between a diploid and a tetraploid. Although they are easy growers with bigger flowers than diploids, they do not usually breed. Triploids are identified by the symbol '3n'.

❀ Tetraploids have four sets of chromosomes. While the flowers of these plants are excellent, they produce fewer of them than either diploids or triploids and tend to be slow growers. Tetraploids are identified by the symbol '4n'.

❀ Aneuploids are plants with odd chromosome counts and are not suitable for breeding at all.

FLASKING

Flasking involves sowing orchid seed in a special gel-based growing mixture. The procedure is not difficult to carry out, but it does require sterile conditions, attention to detail, and certain equipment (see page 63).

It is critical that the seeds are not exposed to any bacteria during the process. In a laboratory, flasking is conducted in an air-flow cabinet to ensure a sterile environment. You can get a similar effect at home by working inside a plastic bag that has been rinsed out with a weak bleach solution. Be sure to wear protective clothing and work with clean latex gloves.

Once the seed is in the flasking jars, store the sealed jars in a draught-free spot with natural light and a constant temperature of 20°C (68°F). (Commercial laboratories usually have a climate-controlled flask house with special lighting.) When the seeds begin to swell and turn light-green, the germination process has begun. Depending on the type of orchid, germination may take from two to three weeks, or several months.

The seeds will not resemble plants for some time, but will continue to swell and develop into small, bright-green masses of plant tissue, called protocorms. Unless the seed was sown very evenly and thinly, the protocorms will need to be replanted, or thinned out. Follow the same process as the original flasking.

After the second flasking, the protocorms produce very fine, thread-like roots that will grow into the agar-based gel in search of nutrients. Tiny leaves will appear shortly after the roots.

Thin out the protocorms one more time using the method previously described. With this flasking, add additional nutrients to the mixture. You can buy ready-made nutrient formula, but adding liquefied fruit, such as bananas or pineapple, will boost the nutrient level as well. Over several months the protocorms will continue to grow and develop into plantlets.

The plantlets are ready to come out of the flask when they have developed roots and some small leaves and are starting to resemble a miniature plant. At this stage, carefully remove them from the agar gel to avoid damaging their fragile roots. Rinse off any remaining gel with tepid water.

Pot the plantlets reasonably close together in a community pot, where they will establish themselves more

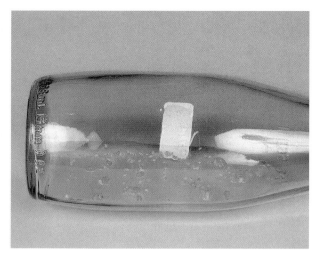

An orchid seed capsule may contain a few or many thousands of seeds. Seed is extremely fine and should be sown when fresh for the best results.

quickly than if they are potted individually. The potting medium should be free-draining and friable (ideally a mix of equal parts seedling grade bark and perlite).

Water the pots when they become slightly dry, but do not allow them to dry out completely, or let the compost remain saturated. Initially, add a mild fungicide to the water. The first days out of the flask are critical and the plants are vulnerable to bacterial infections that can cause them to 'damp off', or rot. The fungicide will help to prevent this disaster.

Keep the plantlets in a humid well-ventilated environment at temperatures ranging from a daytime high of 27°C (80°F) to a night-time low of 18°C (65°F), ideally in a propagator (plant incubator). Refrain from feeding until they have begun to show signs of new growth (up to four weeks after planting). Then offer a weak fertilizer solution as over-feeding can burn soft new growth.

Established plantlets can be potted individually. When they are clearly hardened off and thriving they can be moved to their spot in the greenhouse. It will be several years before they become mature flowering plants. There is a common misconception that orchids flower inconsistently, or only once every seven years. This is untrue, and there is no reason why a plant should not flower every year, given proper care under proper conditions.

After germination PLB's or protocorm-like bodies, small masses of tissue, will form before the roots and leaves begin to emerge.

TISSUE CULTURE PROPAGATION

Tissue culture propagation is a type of vegetative propagation performed at a cellular level. Also called meristem propagation, or mericloning, the process is used by commercial growers to mass-produce genetically identical plants. Although it can be done at home, it really requires sterile laboratory conditions.

At the tip of each new plant growth is a microscopic piece of tissue called the 'apical meristem'. To propogate new plants, the meristem is cut from the plant using a scalpel, and germinated in a nutrient formula in much the same way that seeds are flasked. Within a few weeks, the tissue develops into a globular green mass called a 'protocorm-like body, or 'plb'.

If left to develop fully, the plb will form a plant identical to its parent plant. However, the plb can be divided many times to produce multiple plb's, each of which will develop into a plant that is genetically identical to its parent, thus enabling the large-scale production of plants with specific characteristics. (Mutations sometimes occur, but these plants are culled as soon as they appear, thereby ensuring the integrity of the process.)

In orchid catalogues, seedling and meristem plants are usually listed separately.

FLASKING PROCEDURE

Sowing orchid seeds in a specialized growing medium requires sterile conditions and attention to detail, but is not difficult. Just be sure that you observe the basic steps outlined below.

1 Replated flask:
Sometimes, when the seed has germinated and the protocorms have begun to grow, the plantlets need to be given more space. This process is known as replating.

2 Seedlings ready for removal:
After having been replated the seedlings will begin to grow relatively quickly in their flasks. Once roots and leaves have fully emerged the young seedlings can be removed from the flasks.

3 Community pots:
The agar gel must be washed off once seedlings are removed from the flask. Experience has shown that the seedlings thrive if they are potted close to each other in one pot, known as a 'community' pot.

4 Established community pots:
As soon as the young seedlings are beginning to establish themselves again, remove them from the community pot and pot them individually.

FLASKING EQUIPMENT

✿ Special flasking containers, or any glass jar with well-fitting lid or stopper. Sterilized plastic containers are also available.

✿ Pressure cooker or microwave oven for sterilizing glass containers.

✿ Calcium hyperchlorite or household bleach to sterilize the seed.

✿ Seed nutrient formula: the jelly contains nitrates, phosphates and sulphates with added sugars. Premixed formulas are available from orchid suppliers or chemical companies that specialize in plant formulae.

✿ Distilled or purified water.

✿ A small, sterilized spatula for sowing the seed.

SHOWING YOUR ORCHIDS

For collectors, show time is the highlight of the annual orchid calendar. Hopefully, it is also when most of the plants are in flower, having been primed to perfection throughout the year. As the time approaches, you need to prepare your plants for exhibition.

EARLY PREPARATIONS

As flower stems emerge and mature, protect the buds from slugs, snails and other insects. Mice can be a prob-

Detail of an orchid exhibit by the Eric Young Orchid Foundation.

lem, because they like the warmth of the greenhouse in autumn, winter and early spring. In a greenhouse, food is usually in short supply and the pollen makes a tasty morsel for small rodents. In spring, bumblebees can damage pollen caps and cause early fading or pollination, which will cause the flowers to wither prematurely.

In exhibition orchids the flower stems must be shown off above the foliage, so staking is important. Early staking will prevent the flowers from opening in all directions and encourage a good arrangement of spikes – vital for judging. Place a stake behind the emerging stem and use a simple tie to secure it. Do not truss stems as it takes away their elegance.

By the time it is fully grown, the stem should have two or three ties at most, depending on the length of the inflorescence, and it should not be tied past the first opening flower. Flower heads will become heavier as they open, so support and tie the stem higher up if necessary. Not all stems need to be trained straight; arching stems can be very attractive and are sometimes more elegant.

Training the stems takes time, so be patient. If you are unsure how to go about it, ask a fellow society member to share their experience. Remember to place all your plants facing the same way on the bench, to ensure that the flowers all open in the same direction.

GETTING THE PLANTS READY

Clean each leaf individually and avoid commercial leaf shine products in favour of fresh water or a mix of milk and water to make the leaves glossy. Then clean the pot thoroughly, or use a pot cover or basket if the plant is an individual entry rather than part of a landscaped exhibit where pots should be hidden by a cloth or other foliage plants. A landscaped exhibit requires a focal point, usually centred in the space. If you decide on a theme, make sure that your props complement rather than dominate the exhibit – the orchids must dominate.

SETTING UP AN EXHIBIT

One of the decisions you need to make is how you want to show your orchids. Decide whether to group the plants by genus (e.g. all Paphiopedilums together), or by colour (e.g. all the orange-flowered orchids together). Grouping by colour is often easier for novices who do not want to specialize in a particular genus, or may still be building their collection.

Once the backdrop has been put up, you can begin to build the exhibit, working away from a focal point in the centre towards the outsides and finally putting the finishing touches at the front.

As you assemble your exhibit, stand back periodically to make sure it is coming together with uniformity and elegance. Ensure that the gradations in height are correct from left to right and from back to front. See to it that the best plants are in a prominent position and always allow space between groups of plants so that there is room for the 'butterflies to fly around'.

When you are done with the set-up make any final adjustments and water the exhibit well before you leave after a long day's work. Remember to add signage in the form of your name or some other means of identification.

Adding detail

Choose good foliage plants with unblemished, cleaned leaves to support your orchids. Flowering plants other than orchids are usually not permitted, but check with show officials beforehand if you are unsure.

Exotic bromeliads add a tropical feel, but their flowers may disqualify an exhibit. Green ferns, tree ferns and foliage plants are better than red or tricoloured foliage, which often detracts from rather than enhances the exhibit. Driftwood and green carpet moss are favourites for a natural landscape and are usually readily available from suppliers. Autumn leaves or pine bark make good ground covers that complement a natural exhibit; pebbles and small stones can also be very attractive.

Once set up, the finishing touches are added to the exhibit. This is usually a team effort.

The finished South African exhibit at a World Orchid Show.

JUDGING

Before a show all good societies produce a schedule that contains the rules and regulations set out by the show committee. The schedule will indicate the theme, if there is one, and will also give guidelines on what is and is not permitted for the individual exhibits.

Often, individual plants must be entered before the deadline, which will be indicated on the show schedule. At larger shows, all labelled plants are automatically eligible for competition, so read the schedule carefully and note the procedures. Your exhibit may require a separate entry form, so to check whether you have to enter individual plants as well as the entire exhibit.

The entry system should be clearly explained in the show schedule, but if you have any doubts ask the show manager or stewards, who are there to assist you. There is usually no charge for entry to local or national shows, but check beforehand if you are not sure. Although the paperwork can be tiresome, it is worth the effort. Smaller shows often require less paperwork.

greenhouse environment. It is a good idea to keep a few spare plants on hand for the duration of the show to replenish the exhibit if necessary.

Lighting

Use lighting to focus on individual plants or groups of plants, drawing attention to their special features. But don't over-light the exhibit as this would make it appear bland.

Labelling

Labelling can make or destroy an elegant exhibit. Black card labels are the best. They should measure about 10 x 5cm (4 x 2in) and be neatly written or typed out. (Remember to use waterproof ink.) Gold or white ink works well on black card, but black ink on white card is also acceptable. Don't label every plant, just the most important ones, to guide the judges.

SHOW DAY

Get in early enough to mist the plants, make final adjustments and check that the labels are visible and straight before the judging starts. Mist the entire exhibit regularly to ensure that the plants do not dehydrate, especially if the exhibition hall is air-conditioned or heated. During the show you should constantly maintain the exhibit to ensure the orchids do not stress in any way now that they are out of their humidity and temperature controlled

You should enter as many good plants as you can. Don't be afraid to enter the plants you have nurtured and attended to so well throughout the year – you might just be rewarded with a certificate or even a trophy.

Some shows offer individual judging, affording orchid owners whose collections are too small for a full exhibit an opportunity to enter single plants. In tabletop judging, similar plants compete against each other and no exhibits are presented.

More often than not, orchids are presented in land-scaped exhibits which range from a few elegantly arranged plants to large entries with hundreds of care-fully nurtured orchids. These bigger exhibits compete against others of the same size and type. Provision is made for novices and younger members.

Prizes are usually trophies and certificates but, in some cases, particularly the Japan Grand Prix (JGP), which is held in Tokyo every February, there are large cash prizes to be won.

THE SHOWBOX

Every enthusiast will have an individualized list of 'essential' items that are needed for a show. Here are some of the items you may need:

❁ A 'tool box' containing: spare labels, pens, wire, electrical and masking tape, pliers, hammer, nails, tacks or drawing pins, screw drivers, plugs, flex cables, spare light bulbs, plastic cable ties, nylon fishing line, extra stakes, plastic liners or sheets, bin (garbage) bags, backdrops, bottle containing a water-milk mixture for polishing leaves, scissors, dustpan and brush.

❁ Mist sprayer (labelled with your name).

❁ A trolley for moving plants.

❁ Folding chairs and a small table, as well as a cooler box stocked with food and drink.

SHOW CHECKLIST

One week before the show
- Clean selected plants and foliage
- Prepare crates or boxes to transport plants
- Check lights and replace bulbs if necessary
- Gather all props, stands, backdrops etc.
- Check the contents of your show box

The day before the show
- Final preparation of plants to be exhibited.
- Complete the entry forms and put them in a safe place.
- Prepare and pack plants for transport. (Remember to place them with the spikes all facing the same way and use soft paper between the flowers and stems. Support heavy stems. Don't overload boxes or crates – keep them light enough to carry easily.)
- Pack props and backdrops making sure you can access these boxes first. If possible, send them ahead so you can set up before the plants arrive.
- Check your show box and gather any personal items you may need.
- If you are transporting your plants in warm weather, you may need to shade the vehicle's side windows with sun-screens or paper (ensure your visibility is not impaired). Use the air conditioner to cool the vehicle before packing the plants into it, and throughout the journey.
- If you are transporting your plants in cold weather, you may need to preheat the interior of your vehicle before it is loaded up (allow time for this).

After the show
- Remove labels for reuse. Dispose of foliage plants, moss and dying flowers before taking plants home.
- Put bark chips and other props into bags.
- Remove debris, lift the lining, sweep the area and leave the exhibit space as you found it.
- Remember to take your show box, broom and packaging materials with you.

AWARD SYSTEMS

There are several internationally respected awards pro-grammes that offer orchid professionals and enthusiasts an opportunity to be recognized for their exceptional efforts in orchid culture and breeding. Two of the major orchid bodies are the UK's Royal Horticultural Society (RHS) and the American Orchid Society (AOS). Other international societies include the All Japan Orchid Society (AJOS), Deutsche Orchideen-Gesellschaft (DOG), Japan Grand Prix (JGP), Thai Royal Horticultural Society (TRHS) and the South African Orchid Council (SAOC).

Royal Horticultural Society

The oldest awards body is the highly regarded Royal Horticultural Society, which granted the first orchid award in 1859. The RHS grants awards based on the recommendations of the Orchid Committee, a group of professional orchid judges. Plants are evaluated for excellence and discussed by the judges, who then vote and propose the awards.

Following a tradition that began in 1897, the RHS maintains a permanent record of each award-winning plant in the form of a specially commissioned painting.

The judge's evaluation follows the 'Appreciation Method', which allows for some scope in recognizing not only plants with overall exceptional form and quality, but plants that may have a unique or particular feature, or be the product of a new and successful hybrid.

American Orchid Society

The largest orchid judging institution is the American Orchid Society. The AOS judges work on a points system: out of a possible 100, at least 30 per cent of the final score is granted for flower form, 30 per cent for colour, and the remaining 40 per cent for flower size, arrange-ment, number of flowers and length of stem.

The AOS maintains a permanent photographic record of each award-winning plant. It also publishes *Awards Quarterly*, a comprehensive list of awards.

ROYAL HORTICULTURAL SOCIETY AWARDS

First Class Certificate (FCC/RHS)	For orchids of great excellence'
Award of Merit (AM/RHS)	Orchids which are 'meritorious'
Preliminary Commendation (PC/RHS)	Recognizes 'new orchids of promise'
Cultural Commendation Certificate (CCC/RHS)	For a grower who exhibits 'great cultural skill'

AMERICAN ORCHID SOCIETY AWARDS

First Class Certificate (FCC/AOS)	90–100 points
Award of Merit (AM/AOS)	80–89 points
Highly Commended Certificate (HCC/AOS)	75–79 points
Judges Commendation (JC/AOS)	Plants with distinctive characteristics that fall outside the normal judging criteria
Award of Quality (AQ/AOS)	Recognition of improved quality
Award of Distinction (AD/AOS)	Recognition of new breeding trends
Certificate of Horticultural Merit (CHM/AOS)	Well-grown and flowered plant that contributes to the horticultural aspects of orchidology
Certificate of Botanical Recognition (CBR/AOS)	Rare or unusual plants of botanical interest
Certificate of Cultural Merit (CCM/AOS)	Cultural excellence
Certificate of Cultural Excellence (CCE/AOS)	Further distinction for cultural excellence

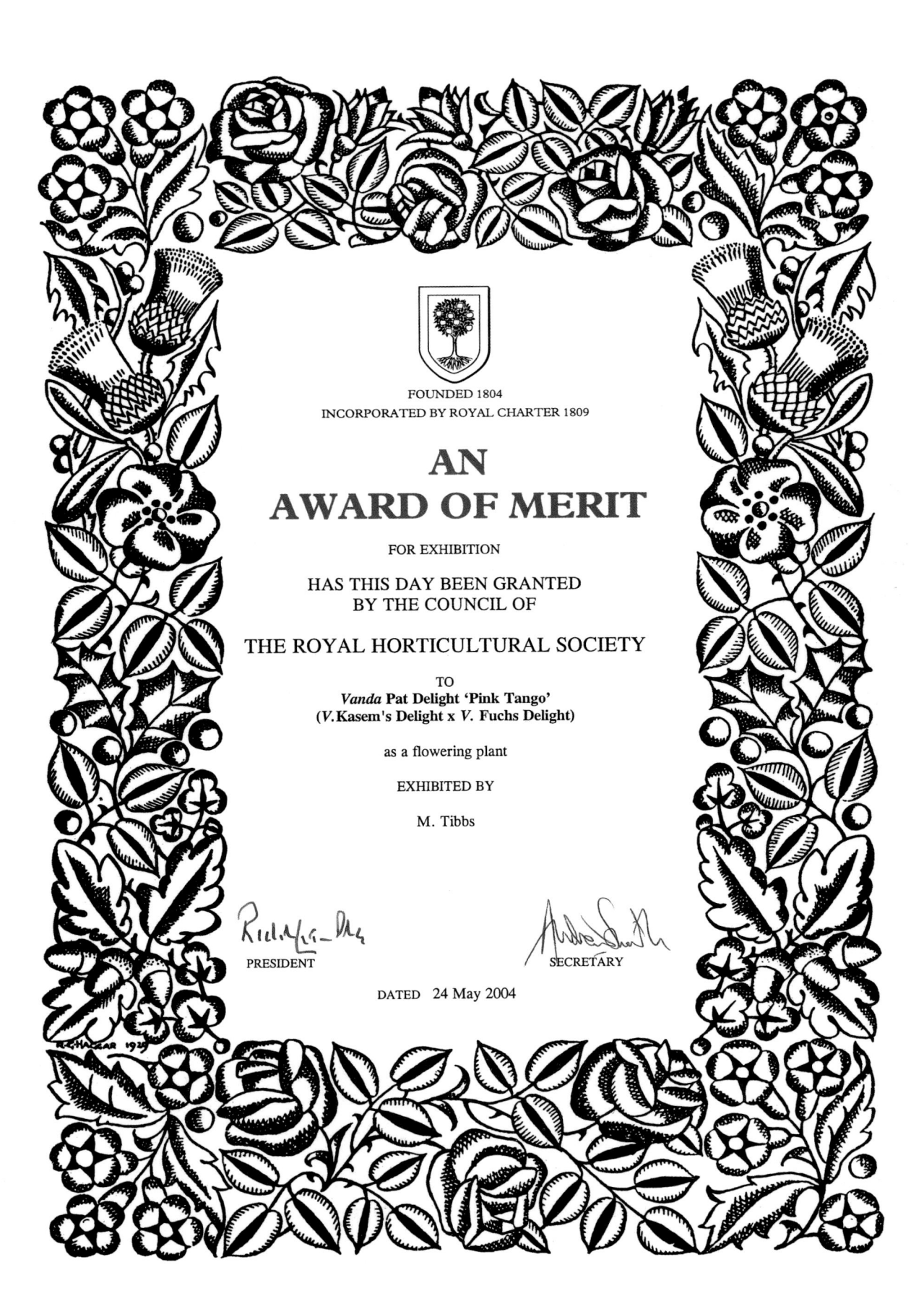

FOUNDED 1804
INCORPORATED BY ROYAL CHARTER 1809

AN
AWARD OF MERIT

FOR EXHIBITION

HAS THIS DAY BEEN GRANTED
BY THE COUNCIL OF

THE ROYAL HORTICULTURAL SOCIETY

TO
Vanda Pat Delight 'Pink Tango'
(*V.* Kasem's Delight x *V.* Fuchs Delight)

as a flowering plant

EXHIBITED BY

M. Tibbs

PRESIDENT

SECRETARY

DATED   24 May 2004

ORCHID CLASSIFICATION

Classification attempts to place together plants that are related to each other in terms of overall similarity, as well as in an evolutionary sense. There are two international bodies that regulate and classify the naming of all plants, including orchids.

The International Code of Botanical Nomenclature (ICBN) is concerned with plants found in the wild. The ICBN code book is revised every five years to include new discoveries or the reclassification of existing plants. The similarly named International Code of Nomenclature for Cultivated Plants (ICNCP) is concerned only with cultivated plants, including cultivars (cultivated varieties) and natural hybrids of major species, and grexes (see page 72) and cultivars of artificially produced hybrids.

Orchid classification is a man-made aid to understanding the many species in the orchid family and putting them into context. Artificial classifications that divide orchids into groups, like terrestrial or epiphyte, cool or warm-growing, and so on, can help the grower to identify unfamiliar plants, as well as providing clues on how to grow and care for a particular plant.

THE USE OF COMMON NAMES

Many orchids have common names that perfectly (and often quaintly) reflect a distinctive characteristic of the plant, making them more user-friendly than the often intimidating botanical names. For example, 'Fly Orchid', an evocative description of this plant's unusual brownish-coloured fly-shaped flower, rolls off the tongue much more easily than *Ophrys insectifera*. However, while the

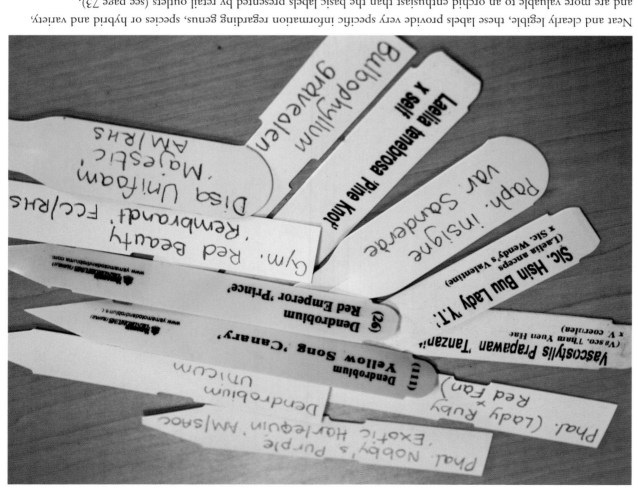

Neat and clearly legible, these labels provide very specific information regarding genus, species or hybrid and variety, and are more valuable to an orchid enthusiast than the basic labels presented by retail outlets (see page 73).

use of common names is perhaps acceptable within one country, where the reference will be understood, a problem arises when information is shared on a global scale.

Many plant species are distributed around the world and so may be known by different common names in various places. Even if a plant is widely known by a single common name, officially recording the numerous translations could be a daunting task. Furthermore, common names do not communicate the specific botanical information that clearly identifies each plant. For this reason, plants are always formally classified by their botanical names which are written in Latin form even when they are derived from another language.

BOTANICAL NAMES

Naming conventions within botanical classifications are based on the binomial system devised by the 18th-century naturalist Carl Linnaeus. The Latin word binomial means two and, simply defined, the system is used to identify all species by a unique name comprised of two classifications: genus and species. Together, these are known as the 'binomial name'. Each species within a genus has a unique name so that it can be distinguished from all other plants in the genus.

Latin has historically been the international language of science and so, while many plant names are based on words that are common in other languages, for scientific and official recording purposes names are 'Latinized' using formal grammatical conventions.

To illustrate the binomial system in its basic form, we use as an example *Dendrobium amethystoglossum*:

- ❀ The genus (generic) name comes first: *Dendrobium*
- ❀ It is followed by a specific epithet (adjective) assigned to the species to identify it: *amethystoglossum*
- ❀ Together they form the proper species name.

The epithet or name given to a species usually describes a characteristic of the plant, such as the flower colour or growth habits. In the case of *Dendrobium amethystoglossum*, it has amethyst-coloured flowers.

To be accepted by the appropriate authorities, a scientific name must be described in a particular way, with

> ### GRAMMATICAL POINTS
>
> - The genus name is always capitalized. It may be abbreviated. (*Dendrobium amethystoglossum* may appear as either *D. amethystoglossum* or *Den. amethystoglossum*, for example.)
>
> - Species and variety names are always in lower case.
>
> - Genus, species and variety names are always italicized.
>
> - 'Variety' or 'form' are written as 'var.' or 'forma' and written in Roman type.
>
> - Grex names (see page 72) are written in Roman type with initial capitalization.
>
> - Cultivar names are written in roman type, with initial capitalization, and enclosed in single quotation marks.
>
> - Awards are abbreviated and appear in capital letters.

a proper Latin description and a type specimen described. A type specimen is a perfect example of the plant that has been preserved and deposited in a herbarium. The name should also appear in a recognized scientific journal, book or other printed matter.

The names of subspecies, varieties and forms are subject to the same rules that govern species, but hybrids are named using a different set of rules which combine the scientific names of both parent plants, using a multiplication sign (x). Generic names for hybrids are the same as those of the parent plants, but when two different genera are crossed the new hybrid name is a combination of the parental genus names.

Newcomers to the world of orchids may find the naming conventions confusing at first, but as you become more familiar with them it will get easier to read and interpret plant labels.

INTERPRETING ORCHID NAMES
Because orchids are extensively bred to develop specific characteristics, their classification is a bit more complex than most other plants. Learning how to interpret orchid names is an important step if you wish to become a serious collector. The basic binomial system has been described on page 71, but most orchids are described by more than just two names.

For example, within a species, a plant may exhibit some characteristics that set it apart from the others, such as a somewhat larger or differently coloured flower. These differences are known as varieties or forms, and are abbreviated in the name as 'var.' or 'f'.

The example *Dendrobium nobile* var. *pendulum* takes the binomial system to the next level:

* ❀ Genus: *Dendrobium*
* ❀ Species: *nobile*
* ❀ Variety: *pendulum*

In this case, the species name describes the flower as *nobile* (noble) and this particular variety as *pendulum* (pendulous or free-swinging). The Latin words are not always so obviously translated, but this is a good illustration of how the naming system works.

The binomial system is the standard by which naturally occurring orchids are identified and classified. With the advent of hybrids (see page 76), classification became even more complicated and a new system was needed to identify hybrids cultivated by commercial growers.

Cultivars
Combining the words 'cultivated' and 'variety', a cultivar is a genetically unique plant that is vegetatively propagated through dividing or cloning, rather than from seed. All of the offspring are genetically identical and therefore share a common cultivar name. Not all cultivars are named, only those plants that show exceptional properties, such as brilliant markings or finely formed petals. Cultivar names are regulated by the International Code of Nomenclature for Cultivated Plants. A typical cultivar name is written as:
Phalaenopsis equestris 'Candor Violette', FCC/AOS.

* ❀ Botanical name: *Phalaenopsis equestris*
* ❀ Cultivar or award name: 'Candor Violette'
* ❀ FCC/AOS indicates that the plant has been awarded a First Class Certificate by the American Orchid Society.

The botanical name appears as is customary and the cultivar name is simply added to it. When written as part of a full plant name, the cultivar name is written in Roman type, with initial capital letters and set within single quotation marks. The plant's awards or recognition are listed at the end and written in capital letters.

Hybrids
A hybrid is a cross between genetically unlike individuals. Orchid hybrids are identified by a 'grex name', which is chosen and registered by the hybridizer. The term grex, which comes from Greek and means 'flock' or 'group', refers to all the offspring as well as subsequent offspring of a hybrid cross.

Produced by seed, and regardless of variations in form or colour, all offspring share a common lineage and are therefore members of a common grex. The cultvars may be given individual names, but the grex name always precedes them.

This example includes a grex name and a cultivar name; *Phalaenopsis* Hilo Lip 'Lovely', as follows:

* ❀ Genus: *Phalaenopsis*
* ❀ Grex: Hilo Lip
* ❀ Cultivar: 'Lovely'

The genus name is italicized, followed by the grex name which is written in Roman type with initial capital letters. The cultivar name, as discussed above, is written in Roman type with initial capitals and enclosed in single quotation marks.

A selection of labels from pot plant suppliers and retail outlets. While these labels stipulate basic requirements of the plants they are not specific about the type of orchid, its correct name, or variety.

Much effort goes into the preparation for a show. Each orchid must be neatly and individually labelled.

Sometimes the parent cross (the plants from which the cultivar was bred) is included in the name, as in the example *Phalaenopsis* 'Southern Ruby' (Lady Ruby x Redfan):

* ❀ Genus: *Phalaenopsis*
* ❀ Cultivar: 'Southern Ruby'
* ❀ Seed parent: Lady Ruby
* ❀ Pollen parent: Redfan

The parent cross is indicated by an 'x'. The seed (male) parent is listed first, followed by the pollen (female) parent. Grex names are registered by the International Orchid Registration Society, part of the Royal Horticultural Society.

Alliances and intergeneric hybrids

When different genera within a single tribe are closely related by common properties and characteristics, they are classified in a grouping called an Alliance. Plants within an Alliance are suitable for breeding, and the progeny are called intergeneric hybrid crosses. These hybrids form a new genus that is identified by a hybrid generic name.

As with a standard generic name, the hybrid generic name appears first: *Doritaenopsis* Red Pearl 'Barbara Ann', AM/AOS.

* ❀ *Doritaenopsis* refers to intergeneric cross between *Doritis* and *Phalaenopsis* (two members of the Phalaenopsis Alliance)
* ❀ Grex: Red Pearl
* ❀ Cultivar: 'Barbara Ann'
* ❀ AM/AOS: Award of Merit from the American Orchid Society.

REGISTRATION OF NEW ORCHID HYBRIDS

The first orchid hybrid register, called *Sander's List*, was published in 1906 by Sander & Sons Orchids of St Albans, UK. In 1962, maintenance and publication of Sander's List was taken over by International Cultivar Registration Authority for Orchid Hybrids, under the aegis of the Royal Horticultural Society.

Orchids are one of the only plant families for which new hybrids and intergeneric hybrids continue to be registered and recorded, and *Sander's List* remains an international authoritative source of record. The register is available from the RHS in book form and on CD-Rom.

The Royal Horticultural Society has been recording hybrids in the International Orchid Register since the first orchids were crossed in 1854.

At current estimates, some 110,000 hybrids (also called grexes) have been registered from the almost 25,000 known species. Current registration regulations and application forms are easily accessed via the Royal Horticultural Society's web site (see page 154). For research purposes, you may search the hybrid registration database by both parentage and grex name.

APPLICATION FOR REGISTRATION OF AN ORCHID HYBRID

P:	T:	Registrar's use only

(Before filling in this form please consult the notes overleaf. Use block capitals or typescript.)

Your ref/seedling no.*

PAYMENT MUST ACCOMPANY THE APPLICATION

I enclose cheque* / RHS credit note* for £7.50* / US$12.50*
OR
Debit £7.50 from my American Express* / Visa* / Mastercard* / Diners* credit card

No:

*delete those not applicable

Expiry date

GREX

GENUS -

GREX EPITHET (1ST CHOICE) -

GREX EPITHET (2ND CHOICE) -

TWO CHOICES **MUST** BE GIVEN

DATE OF MAKING CROSS (ie. pollination)

DATE OF FIRST FLOWERING

see Note 6 overleaf

BRIEF DESCRIPTION OF FIRST FLOWERS - see overleaf to continue

PARENTS

SEED ♀ | POLLEN ♂

GENUS: | GENUS:

EPITHET: | EPITHET:
Specific or Grex Epithet | *Specific or Grex Epithet*

EPITHET: | EPITHET:
Varietal or Cultivar Epithet (Optional) | *Varietal or Cultivar Epithet (Optional)*

APPLICANT

TITLE: | FORENAMES:

SURNAME: | OR TRADING NAME:

ADDRESS:

POSTCODE: | COUNTRY:

FAX/PHONE (optional): | E-MAIL (optional):

I do / do not*
authorise the disclosure of parental cultivar epithets
*delete as appropriate

Colour photograph enclosed?
Yes/No*
*delete as appropriate
(see Note 7 overleaf)

Applicant's declaration regarding originator

Either (1)   I am the Originator as defined in Note 5 overleaf .... ☐
Or (2)   The Originator is unknown as explained by me overleaf .... ☐
Or (3)   The Originator's name and address is:

_____

_____

and (a)   has given permission for this application .... ☐
or (b)   is no longer extant, has no living spouse and no assignee is known to me .... ☐
or (c)   has not replied to any written request for permission
                 as sent to him on .... (date - over 3 months ago) ☐
                                                        ONE BOX ABOVE MUST BE TICKED

I certify to the best of my knowledge and belief the particulars and declaration given above are correct. I agree to my personal details being kept on record.

Signature of applicant . . . . Date. . . . .
NO APPLICATION CAN BE ACCEPTED UNLESS ALL THE DECLARATIONS ABOVE ARE COMPLETED

To register a new hybrid, this form must be completed and forwarded to the registrar in the United Kingdom, where all records of hybrid orchids are maintained by the Royal Horticultural Society. Forms are available online.

Orchid hybrids

Cool-climate orchids

As the term implies, cool-growing orchids originate in temperate climates and at high elevations where they are frequently cooled by cloud cover, but they also do well in warmer conditions.

Native to a vast area from China to northern Australia, Cymbidiums have been hybridized and now comprise one of the biggest sections of the pot plant and cut-flower markets. Odontoglossums and Masdevallias originate in the higher reaches of the Andes mountains in South America where the plants are cooled by moist clouds in the late afternoon. Odontoglossums cross-breed easily with warmer-growing Oncidiums, thus allowing collectors in warmer areas the opportunity to enjoy plants from the cooler regions.

Disas grow naturally in the mountainous regions of South Africa's Western Cape province, in particular on Table Mountain in Cape Town. Here, the plants experience cool winds all year round with cold rain and occasional snowfalls in winter. Summer temperatures are high, but the plants' roots are kept cool by fresh mountain streams. Provided they are protected from frost they can survive in temperatures of 6–8°C (43–46°F) without risk of damage.

PREVIOUS PAGES (MAIN IMAGE) *Dendrobium* Hans Neuerhaus.
OPPOSITE *Dracula robledorum* 'Tapestry'.

CYMBIDIUM

Origin	Southeast Asia; Himalayas to China, Japan; Philippines to New Guinea, northern/eastern Australia
Min/max temps	10–30°C (50–85°F)
Flowers	Late summer to spring, depending on hybrid; large, standard, intermediate or miniature
Light	Provide good light, but no direct sun (30–40% shading)
Feeding	Hungry feeders
Pronunciation	sim–bid–ee–um

Cym. Candy King (Valley King x Candy Floss) 'Jane'.

Cym. Crash Landing (Rio Rita x Red Beauty).

CULTIVATION

Cymbidium species are not widely cultivated except by a few hobbyists, but hybrids have been developed for decades and are among some of the most popular orchids, as pot plants and cut flowers. They come in a full range of colours, and their good clear hues have richly spotted or blotched markings on the lip. Flowers are long-lasting – at least six weeks when cut, and up to 10 weeks on the plant. The plants have been developed in large, standard, intermediate and miniature forms.

Cymbidiums originate from Southeast Asia, the Himalayas, China and Japan, but are known to extend as far south as Australia's Northern Territory. Hybrids are extensively grown throughout Europe and the USA.

The plants are typically glossy in their appearance and have been developed with some degree of warmth tolerance, which enables them to flower from late summer right through to late spring. Conveniently, their main flowering period coincides with the Christmas season in the northern hemisphere.

Temperature

Cymbidiums are cool growers, but that does not mean they won't grow in warmer climates or heated homes. In warm temperatures, the flowers will generally not last as long as if they were kept in cooler conditions. Cymbidiums enjoy an ideal temperature range of between 10–30°C (50–85°F) and may stress at temperatures above or below this range. However, in late summer they need a drop in night temperature to initiate flowering stems. This drop is essential to ensure maximum flowering. The buds can turn yellow and fall from the stems if the plants get too warm at night, so ensure they are kept cool until the flowers have opened.

Light

These orchids enjoy good light. Indoors they should be situated out of direct light, but near a good source of natural light, while in a greenhouse they require enough shade in summer to avoid scorching the leaves. Good light will ensure that the plants are hardened and do not have soft lanky growth reaching for the light. Hardened plants flower more successfully and produce strong, firm stems to carry the heavy flower heads.

Water and humidity

During the flowering season water the plants regularly to the point of being damp only; they do not like being saturated or left standing in water. This can cause the roots to rot and decay, eventually killing the plant.

Indoors, stand the Cymbidiums in a planter deep enough to hold 2–3cm (1–2in) of pebbles or gravel to create the humidity that is essential for them (the gravel should never be submerged). Humidity prevents crinkled leaves, a sure sign that the plant is dehydrated. Greenhouse plants can be watered overhead or with a lance that will also serve to wash dust from the leaves and keep the plants in good condition. Air movement is vital, but do not confuse it with cold draughts. The bigger the area around the plants, the more air movement there will be and the sooner they will dry out.

Feeding

Cymbidiums are hungry feeders. If they are not fed adequately they will not flower well or the flowers will be pale and sparse on weak stems. A high nitrogenous fertilizer (such as 30:10:10) should be used in spring to encourage new growth; this can be changed to more general 18:18:18 feed for the summer. In autumn a high potash-based fertilizer (10:30:20) will induce flowering, but change this to half-strength general feed throughout the winter. Feed at least once a week, ensuring that they are watered well enough to rinse out any excess salts from the fertilizer. A build-up of undissolved fertilizer in the potting medium can burn new roots and cause rotting.

Pests and diseases

Outdoors, and after flowering, Cymbidiums will survive happily in a semi-shaded spot or under a tree, but a careful spraying programme must be followed as the plants will become more susceptible to pests and diseases than if they remained in a greenhouse or inside the home.

Orchids are as susceptible as any other plant when it comes to pests, and unless you have a quarantine area it is difficult to protect them. Cymbidiums are prone to red spider mite and scale insects. They can also be attacked by the Cymbidium mosaic virus (see page 43), an incurable virus that discolours the leaves and leads to deformed and irregular colouration in the flowers. Infected plants must be destroyed.

POTTING MIX AND REPOTTING

Cymbidiums are best repotted in the spring after they have flowered and this must be done at least every second year. There are various potting media options (see page 55) to choose from – the most popular is a mixture of equal parts medium-grade bark and perlite.

Various additions can be made to the basic potting mix. Peat or coconut fibre can be incorporated, provided some dolomitic lime is added to neutralize their high acidic content. Rockwool is quite popular, but it is unsightly and can irritate unprotected skin. Diatomaceous earth added to rockwool mixes has proved to be more stable than rockwool on its own.

Horticultural-grade foam chips are another addition to rockwool that will help to keep the mixture aerated and prevent it from compacting. Rockwool mixes must never be allowed to dry out as they are difficult to re-wet without using a wetting agent.

ODONTOGLOSSUM ALLIANCE

Origin	At high altitudes in Central & South America (Mexico and Guatemala to Peru and Brazil)
Min/max temps	10–24°C (50–75°F)
Flowers	At various times; flowers last up to eight weeks
Light	Prefers shade, no direct sun (60–70% shade cloth)
Feeding	Light feeders; water lightly and frequently; challenging to grow
Pronunciation	oh–don–toe–glossum

Odm. (Samares x Augres) 'Summer Snow'.

Odontoglossums were some of the first orchid species imported from the high peaks of the Andes for cultivation in Europe. Because of the lack of knowledge at the time, tens of thousands of these beautiful, cool-growing orchids perished in balmy stove-houses. Eventually, collectors got the cultivation right and many elegant species are today widely grown, especially *Odontoglossum crispum* and *O. nobile* (syn. *O. pescatorei*). The name Odontoglossum is derived from the Latin *odont* (tooth) and *glossum* (pertaining to the tongue), and a 'toothed tongue' or frilly lip is easily observed on the flower.

Odontoglossums breed easily with allied genera and many intergeneric hybrids have been produced with their main breeding partners – *Brassia*, *Cochlioda*, *Miltonia* and *Oncidium*. The resulting progeny can exhibit unique forms and colours that have, over the years, caused quite a stir among collectors. Generally, the goal in hybridizing with allied genera is to add some warmth-tolerance into this family of orchids to make them easier to grow.

There are some 300 species in this subtribe, many of which have been separated from the genus Odontoglossum into their own unique genera or sub-genera. Although the species are still closely allied, they have become botanically differentiated by their specific make-up, habitat or location. This process of revision is ongoing. For the sake of simplicity, this book will not stand on botanical ceremony, but will maintain the name Odontoglossum for species that have been recently moved or are currently under review.

Odontoglossums flower in a kaleidoscope of colours, in particular clear whites and sunny yellows. Flower stems from a mature bulb are usually produced singly and carry from eight to ten sizable flowers that last up to six weeks. The plants are generally compact, producing a fairly large glossy pseudobulb and a pair of ovate leaves. Flower spikes emerge from the base of a mature bulb at almost any time of the year, but there is no doubt that flowers produced in the cooler months are superior to those produced in the summer. While they have been developed over time as pot plants, they do not possess long-lasting qualities as cut flowers.

CULTIVATION
Odontoglossums are slightly more difficult to grow than other orchids and stress more easily if the correct growing conditions are not provided.

Temperature
Odontoglossums thrive in temperatures from 10°C (50°F) as a low night-time temperature and up to 24°C (75°F) as an ideal daytime high. They will survive in temperatures slightly below or above the ideal, but may suffer stress. When the outside temperature is low, keep the plants a little drier as their roots can rot easily. If this happens they will regress and be difficult to keep alive.

When temperatures are too high, Odontoglossums should be kept in shade and their leaves misted lightly to reduce their temperature and alleviate the loss of moisture. Dehydration is easily observed on the bulbs which will show signs of wrinkling. Bulbs will also shrivel if the plant is permitted to flower in summer, when it is most likely to suffer from stress. If the leaves become extremely red or develop intense red pigmentations as summer progresses, extra shade should be offered.

Light, water and humidity
Odontoglossums like a shaded spot in the greenhouse or home and must be kept out of direct sunlight. Greenhouses should be heavily shaded to prevent the sun from scorching their leaves and prevent excessive dehydration. Ideally, they prefer a climatically controlled environment and can prove difficult to grow in a shade house unless good shading and adequate humidity can be maintained.

Odm. Somelle (Moselle x Golden Ransom) 'Golden Days'.

Humidity is vital to the survival of this species and so is good air movement. Humidity can be introduced by spraying under the greenhouse benches every two to three hours in the summer, less as winter approaches. Indoors, humidity can be maintained by standing the plants on a damp pebble tray and misting during the heat of the day. Check that the leaves are erect and firm – pleated leaves indicate a lack of humidity.

Odontoglossums like to be watered lightly and often from overhead rather than being drenched and left to stand in damp compost. Long wet spells can easily cause rotting of the thin roots. Allow the water to permeate downward and let the compost become almost dry before lightly watering again. This can be done daily if the growing medium has sufficiently dried, or every two days in the winter.

POPULAR ODONTOGLOSSUM/ONCIDIUM ALLIANCE INTERGENERIC HYBRIDS

INTERGENERIC NAME	ABBREVIATION	GENERA CROSSES THAT CREATE THE HYBRID
Alexanderara	(Alxra.)	= Odontoglossum x Brassia x Cochlioda x Oncidium
Aliceara	(Alcra.)	= Oncidium x Brassia x Miltonia
Bakerara	(Bak.)	= Oncidium x Brassia x Miltonia x Odontoglossum
Beallara	(Bllra.)	= Odontoglossum x Brassia x Cochlioda x Miltonia
Burrageara	(Burr.)	= Odontoglossum x Cochlioda x Miltonia x Oncidium
Charlesworthara	(Cha.)	= Oncidium x Cochlioda x Miltonia
Colmanara	(Colm.)	= Odontoglossum x Miltonia x Oncidium
Degamoara	(Dgmra.)	= Odontoglossum x Brassia x Miltonia
Goodaleara	(Gdlra.)	= Oncidium x Odontoglossum x Brassia x Miltonia x Cochlioda
MacLellenara	(McLna.)	= Odontoglossum x Brassia x Oncidium
Miltassia	(Mtssa.)	= Brassia x Miltonia
Miltonidium	(Mtdm.)	= Miltonia x Oncidium
Odontioda	(Oda.)	= Odontoglossum x Cochlioda
Odontobrassia	(Odbrs.)	= Odontoglossum x Brassia
Odontocidium	(Odcdm.)	= Odontoglossum x Oncidium
Odontonia	(Odtna.)	= Odontoglossum x Miltonia
Oncidioda	(Oncda.)	= Oncidium x Cochlioda
Sanderara	(Sand.)	= Odontoglossum x Brassia x Cochlioda
Vuylstekeara	(Vuyl.)	= Odontoglossum x Cochlioda x Miltonia
Wilsonara	(Wils.)	= Oncidium x Cochlioda x Odontoglossum

Feeding

Odontoglossums cannot tolerate strong fertilizers which can burn their fine roots and damage the developing bulbs. They thrive on a low concentration or weak fertilizer. Like Cymbidiums, they prefer a high nitrogenous fertilizer in spring to support and encourage new growth, followed by a general feed in summer and a high potash-based fertilizer in the autumn. In winter, a weak general feed may be offered to sustain the flowering stems.

POTTING MIX AND REPOTTING

The best compost for Odontoglossums is a mix of equal parts of peat, perlite and seedling bark. Sphagnum moss can be substituted for the peat. Bark and coarse perlite will ensure a well-drained base and peat or sphagnum moss will hold moisture from the frequent showers of water.

When using peat, add a large handful of powdered dolomitic lime to every 50 litres (11 gal) of total mix. This will ensure that the peat, which is slightly acidic, is neutralized and will create a more stable compost. Rockwool and horticultural foam have also been used extensively; mixes of coconut fibre and bark have had some success. Odontoglossums must be repotted annually as bark, peat and sphagnum moss break down and rot with frequent watering and feeding, particularly in warm climates. When repotting, be sure that a healthy root system is disturbed as little as possible. Remove any damaged or rotten roots and repot using the smallest pot possible.

DISA UNIFLORA AND ITS HYBRIDS

Origin	Tropical and South Africa and Madagascar
Min/max temps	4–30°C (39–85°F)
Flowers	During summer; blooms last up to 10 weeks
Light	Prefer diffused light, with 50–70% shading
Feeding	Replenish trays with very cold, fresh tap water
Pronunciation	dee–za

Relatively new to the cultivated orchid scene, Disas were – until recently – noted for being notoriously difficult to grow. They are very distinctive, with vibrant colours, long lasting flowers, and a triangular shape that makes them look like anything but a typical orchid.

The most widely grown species originates in South Africa. *Disa uniflora* (syn. *Disa grandiflora*) is only found on Cape Town's Table Mountain and surrounding areas. Although the name 'uniflora' suggests that the plant should only produce one flower, the species clearly does not have a single-flowered stem. Disas are generally small in stature, while the flowering stems can reach 1m (3.3ft) in height. Many hybrids are available that easily and quickly mature from seed. Colours vary from simple baby pinks through to vibrant postbox reds, golden yellows and sunny orange hues.

In the wild, the plants grow along small rivers and cold streams, making their home in the roots of reeds, which provide thick mats of tangled fibres in which the Disas embed their roots.

In summer, Disas can become quite dry, in contrast to winter when the plants can survive submerged in cold running water for short periods. In some areas, Disas are covered in snow for short periods without ill effect. Unlike most orchids, Disas thrive in damp, cool conditions and flower in summer, when the weather is normally dry. The Western Cape enjoys a Mediterranean climate that is characterized by cool and wet winters, and hot, dry summers.

Disa Watsonii (*uniflora* x Kewensis).

Disa Unifoam 'Majestic' AM/RHS (*uniflora* x Foam).

CULTIVATION

Over the years, many mistruths have circulated about the cultivation of Disas all of which have been dispelled. As long as a few simple guidelines are followed the plants can be successfully cultivated.

Temperature

Disas make good companions to Cymbidiums and Odontoglossums and are best suited to greenhouse cultivation, but will grow in shade houses and outdoors. They can tolerate a low winter temperature of 4–5°C (39–41°F), and a maximum of 30°C (85°F) in summer. Exposure at either end of this range will cause the plants to suffer. High humidity and very hot summer temperatures are disastrous unless the plants are protected by air conditioning or wet-wall cooling systems.

Light, water and humidity

Although Disas grow naturally in strong light they will be happier if they are protected with some shading in the summer, such as 40–50% shade cloth suspended as high as possible above the plants. Air movement is of prime importance for healthy Disas growing in an enclosed environment or controlled greenhouse. Ventilation will keep bacterial rot at bay and dry any excess water from the foliage. In summer, greenhouse air vents should be opened fully to take advantage of fresh air. Indoors, particularly if the plant is kept in a small, poorly ventilated room, an oscillating fan will provide air movement.

If there is any secret to growing Disas successfully it is constant replenishment of fresh cold water. Disas are best grown standing in trays of water – stagnant water can become smelly and algae can form easily, especially in summer. A good watering regime is to fill the tray at the beginning of the week, add fresh water mid-week and fertilizer in the latter part of the week before draining the tanks at the end of the week and refilling with fresh water. Fertilizer can happily stay in the tank for a couple of days before being drained away. Avoid getting water on the leaves, and maintain a water level halfway up the pots. Tap water can be used without any negative effect, but rainwater is preferable as it contains fewer chemicals. De-ionized water can also be used, but this is not really necessary unless the quality of the available water is very poor.

Plastic pots are best and trays can be simply constructed by lining a solid container with plastic or polythene. The trays should be cleaned when the plants are repotted after flowering, and rinsed with fresh water to remove any slime or algae.

Feeding

The feeding regime that should be followed for Disas is the same as for Odontoglossums (see page 84).

MAINTENANCE AND REPOTTING

After flowering, or if the stems have been cut, the rosette from which the flowering stem emerged will begin to yellow and the plant will appear to die off. This is not uncommon so do not be alarmed. Allow the stem to rot at the base but don't remove it. You can cut it down with a clean, sterilized blade, but leaving the stem to rot allows natural bacteria to form which encourages the growth of plantlets at the base of the plant.

Removing the stem will result in bacterial infections and the plant is likely to perish. When the young plantlets have hardened, remove them and separate them from the original pot. The plantlets are vegetative forms identical to the mother plant.

Large established plants produce stolons and tubers from which new plants will grow. Allow the new plants to emerge from the compost before splitting them off from the main plant. The tubers will shrivel once the plant is established, as they are merely a source of sustenance for the developing plant. As long as the potting medium shows no signs of rotting or decay, the healthy root ball can simply be wrapped with fresh sphagnum moss and placed in a slightly larger pot.

Sphagnum moss is the best medium in which to cultivate Disas. Additions of perlite and peat have met with some success and sharp sand was used prior to moss, but none of the alternatives has proved as successful as sphagnum moss.

Disa Kewensis (*uniflora* x *tripetaloides*).

Disa Allan Graham 'Harry's Dad' HCC/SAOC.

PLEIONE

Origin	East and Southeast Asia, particularly Formosa, China, the Himalayas
Min/max temps	6–24C° (42–78°F)
Flowers	In spring/summer lasting several weeks
Light	50–60% shade
Feeding	Medium feeders; easy to grow; repot annually for best results
Pronunciation	plea–oh–knee

Pleione formosana var. *alba* 'Snow White'.

Pleiones are terrestrial, temperate plants that thrive in cool conditions. They originate from the cool climates in Asia, particularly Taiwan (ROC), China and the Himalayas where their habitats are mainly rocky outcrops. Pleiones occur mostly in pink and white, although a rare species does flower brilliantly yellow. Hybrids have brought a range of new hues from whites through to pinks and yellows to deep apricot tones.

These fascinating little orchids are easy to grow and can be cultivated on a cool north-facing windowsill in the northern hemisphere, or in a cold frame or cold greenhouse that is protected from deep frosts. Pleiones are truly miniature orchids and are cultivated by many plant growers and collectors other than orchid specialists. Collectors of alpine plants usually have them in their plant collections.

Pleione Vesuvius (*bulbocodiides* x *confusa*).

CULTIVATION

During the winter months, the squat conical bulbs shed their leaves and become dormant. When the warmth of spring has arrived, the bulbs will begin to produce small new growths at the base. At this point, the bulbs should be repotted into a mix of peat and coarse grit in a shallow pot or pan that is large enough to comfortably allow for the year's growth and the number of bulbs, but not be too large or too deep.

To pot, remove dead root material and press the bulbs firmly into the dampened mix. New roots will be encouraged as the mix dries. Water carefully – don't drench the compost, merely keep it damp. Avoid getting water into the new growths, especially when temperatures are still very cool, as this can cause bacterial rot. Good air movement is important to remove bacteria and fungal spores harboured in stale, stagnant air. As new growth emerges the flower bud will be formed. It is necessary to feed the Pleiones with a fertilizer high in nitrogen to support this new growth and the emerging buds. The plants will flower in the spring and the flowers can

last several weeks. Mostly single, but occasionally double flowers are borne on a spindly short stem. When flowering is over, continue feeding the plants so that enough sustenance is available to fully replenish the maturing bulbs. Any recommended fertilizer will do, applied according to the manufacturers' instructions.

As autumn temperatures begin to drop, the leaves will show signs of ageing by turning brown and eventually falling off. This is a signal that the Pleione bulbs are ready for their winter rest period. They can be left in the pots or removed and stored in dry paper bags in a cool place. If they are left in their pots, ensure that they stay dry during the winter. Pleiones should be repotted each year for the best results.

Temperature

The ideal winter temperature for Pleiones is 6°C (42°F), though slightly cooler but frost-free conditions will not damage the bulbs. The plants will stress in summer temperatures exceeding much over 26°C (78°F).

TERRESTRIAL ORCHIDS

Origin	Widely distributed
Min/max temps	Min/max temps: 4–30°C (39–85°F)
Flowers	Flowers in spring/summer and some species have jewelled foliage
Light	Prefer semi shade (50% shading)
Feeding	Light feeders; easy to grow in temperate climate gardens; almost all deciduous

Until recently, terrestrial orchids were thought to be absolutely impossible to grow, but they can now be found at garden centres throughout Europe where they are sold as companion plants. They grow extremely well in temperate gardens but can be a trial to raise in warmer climates, although some collectors have had remarkable success with Calanthes from Japan just by cultivating them under the benches in cool-house conditions. A few examples of terrestrials are given below, although most are not well known. However Disas, which are included in this category, are now widely grown and have therefore been covered separately (see pages 85–87).

CYPRIPEDIUM (sip-ree-ped-ium)
Native to the Far East, these orchids can be cultivated with ease on home patios, alongside such plants as Camellias, Rhododendron and Oriental Cymbidium.

Trade in all of these species is restricted by CITES (see page 152) although a few German growers have hybridized *Cypripediums* and offer the hybrids for sale.

ORIENTAL CYMBIDIUM
Highly prized in the Far East, Oriental Cymbidiums (sim-bid-ee-ums) fetch unusually high prices for their rare and strange colour forms. They are not necessarily only desired for their flowers but also for their many different variegated forms of foliage.

DIURIS AND PTEROSTYLIS
(die-ooh-ree-us; tero-sty-lis) The Australian *Diuris* and *Pterostylis* species are often well-cultivated, but little is known about them outside Australasia.

JEWEL ORCHIDS
Many species of *Goodyera* (good-year-a) and *Ludisia* (loo-dis-ee-a) are highly sought-after for their beautiful foliage (their blooms being relatively insignificant compared with the glittering veined foliage). Unlike most terrestrial orchids, these two genera do not have tubers or rhizomes, instead producing creeping stolons (leafy growths). *Ludisia discolor* is especially sought-after, as it is easy to grow and will quickly establish into a big specimen.

EPIPACTIS (epi-pact-us)
Widespread in southern England where it is commonly found in gardens, it is often listed in alpine plant catalogues along with *Dactylorhiza* species. Less common are the *Ophrys* (or bumblebee orchid) and *Orchis* species, which can still be seen growing along the South Downs in England in late spring. They are also found in the Mediterranean and on some of the Greek islands.

SPIRANTHES (spy-ran-thees)
Spiranthes sinensis is an extremely common terrestrial that seeds itself very easily. In Dutch nurseries it can often be found among cut-flower *Paphiopedilum* and *Cymbidium* plants.

CULTIVATION

Nearly all the terrestrials are deciduous. The plants dessicate during summer when much of the growth activity that occurs after flowering takes place underground, forming the tuber which will carry the plant through the winter. Most terrestrials produce small corms or tubers that will sprout in the early spring. Although this is not common in every case, it is a good generalization. Flowers always appear from a matured rosette of leaves on an erect stem.

Terrestrials will grow well in pots in a mixture of washed river sand or grit, leaf mould and loam. Seedling bark and some bone meal may be added, but the pH of the mix should be slightly acidic. Keep the pot damp throughout the year and in a semi-shaded position.

Feeding

Terrestrial orchids are not very heavy feeders. Throughout spring, summer and into early autumn, you should feed them once per week with a half-strength fertilizer solution or an organic feed. No fertilizer is recommended in the late autumn or cold winter months when the plant is dormant.

POPULAR TERRESTRIALS

Cypripedium japonicum
Diuris
Pterostylis
Ludisia discolor (jewel orchid)
Goodyera (jewel orchid)
Epipactis gigantea
Dactylorhiza maculata
Spiranthes sinensis

Ludisia discolor grown into an exceptional specimen.

ZYGOPETALUM

Origin	South America
Min/max temps	10–30°C (50–85°F)
Flowers	Flowers year round; excellent companions to *Cymbidiums*
Light	Require good light, but no direct sun; (40% shade)
Feeding	Hungry feeders
Pronunciation	zy–go–pet–a–lum

Zygopetalums, which originate from the cooler regions of South America, are excellent companion plants to Cymbidiums. They have heavily fragrant flowers in shades of rich olive greens and deep purples and, unlike Cymbidiums, they flower year-round.

Zygopetalum Inky Dink.

Zygopetalums require the same growing conditions and feeding regimes as Cymbidiums. They also suffer from similar ailments. Their leaves are susceptible to black streaking, commonly known as ticking, which can make the plants unsightly. This condition is normally caused by being grown in an overly warm environment.

Within this genus many new hybrids are emerging, especially from Australia. Some of the new intergeneric hybrids, which come in shades of violet, pink, brown and khaki, can be a little tricky for novices to grow.

Unlike many intergeneric hybrids, *Colax* and *Lycaste* are the genera most commonly used to breed with Zygopetalums. While they will interbreed, these genera are different enough to make them somewhat incompatible.

DENDROBIUM

Origin	Widely distributed in Asia, Australia and the southwest Pacific islands
Min/max temps	Cool-growing 10–24°C (50–75°F); intermediate 14–26°C (58–79°F); warm 16–30°C (62–86°F)
Flowers	Various times of the year
Light	Bright light required
Feeding	Must be fed regularly
Pronunciation	den–dro–bee–um

Dendrobium cuthbertsonii.

Dendrobiums comprise the second biggest group of orchids after Bulbophyllums. The family is vast, consisting of over 1,000 species that are widely distributed from India, east to Japan and south through the Philippines, Malaysia, Papua New Guinea, the Polynesian islands and as far south as Australia and even New Zealand. The genus is so variable it is sometimes hard to consider that its members are all related. They are mostly epiphytes but can also be found growing as lithophytes on rocky outcrops.

Because of their wide distribution, Dendrobiums fall into many climatic zones. Many are tropical, but some prefer intermediate conditions and others cooler climates. Most important for all of them is good light.

Dendrobium farmeri.

Dendrobiums will happily tolerate a very bright aspect in any climate. All Dendrobiums possess some form of a pseudobulb, from long and thin to fat and succulent, some are erect while others are pendulous. The flowers also vary in shape and size, and occur in almost every colour imaginable.

COOL-GROWING SPECIES

These species, which include miniature Dendrobiums from New Guinea, such as *Dendrobium cuthbertsonii*, will thrive in warm climates under cool conditions, or in tropical climates in controlled greenhouse conditions. These delightful gems can be easily cultivated in front or near to a cooling system or air conditioner. Flowers come in shades ranging from yellow to orange and pinks to reds, in bicoloured or two-toned patterns. In nature these miniature orchids, not much more than 5cm (2in) in height, can be found growing on tree ferns at elevations where there is occasional good cool cloud cover.

CULTIVATION

Dendrobium cuthbertsonii can successfully be grown in small pots, on slabs of osmunda, or rafts of tree fern fibre. They require regular watering and frequent weak solutions of a general feed.

High humidity is essential to ensure the little bulbs are kept plump. Another interesting cool growing species is *Dendrobium bellatulum*, which comes from India. Also found at high elevations, this plant can tolerate temperatures as low as 8°C (48°F).

INTERMEDIATE-GROWING SPECIES

There are many intermediate-growing species and hybrids, of which the stunning *nobile*-type Dendrobium is one. This group of orchids originates from the Himalayas but has been popularized in Hawaii and Japan by the Yamamoto family, and is more often than not referred to as Yamamoto Dendrobiums. The tall-stemmed bulbs produce flowers in abundance in the spring after the plants have been left to dry through the cool winter months. Unusually, even the old canes or bulbs can produce flowers.

CULTIVATION

These plants have a very vigorous growing season from late spring and throughout the summer when the new growths emerge from the base of the plant and mature quickly. At this time, the plant requires constant watering and feeding to help mature the growths quickly and make the canes or pseudobulbs fat and succulent. The stems are usually heavy and need to be secured and supported vertically.

In autumn, as the temperatures begin to fall, a high potash-based fertilizer should be administered and the plants left in the driest part of the greenhouse. Buds will emerge from almost every node along the swollen canes. If the plant is watered now, it will begin its natural growth cycle; the emerging buds will develop into little plants and few or no flowers will form. It is vital to keep the plants dry until the flowers open.

Although the *Dendrobium nobile* group are intermediate to warm growers, they do enjoy cool dry winters. If temperatures drop too low the plant will cope, but the leaves may yellow and fall off, leaving bare canes. During winter, the most vital factor is light, which the plant requires to maximize flower production. You will be well rewarded for your efforts, as the flowers are long-lasting and quite exceptional in their range of colours.

Repotting is required soon after flowering and this will lead to an active growth period. Old canes can be removed if necessary and laid on damp, washed river sand where, over the summer, the bulbs will produce new *keikis* (see page 59) that can be removed at the end of the growing season and planted. The young plants will be identical to the parent and although they will take a couple of years to mature this is an inexpensive way to increase your collection.

WARMER-GROWING SPECIES

The warmer, more tropical Dendrobiums include the related 'antelope' and *Phalaenopsis* types. The antelope types have dominant erect spiraling petals, while *Phalanopsis* are named because their round, full flowers resemble those of the genus *Phalaenopsis*. Apart from a physical resemblance, however, the two are not related.

CULTIVATION

These Dendrobiums have tall erect canes that are better able to support themselves than the *Dendrobium nobile* types. The pseudobulbs are rigid and carry six pairs of succulent but firm leaves on the top of the bulb. The flowers are usually borne along the mature canes, and are usually spectacular and very long-lasting. Well-grown plants produce stems of flowers from the sides of the pseudobulbs as well as from mature canes.

Humidity is important, as is light, and these plants really do thrive in hot, tropical conditions. The plants are strong and require adequate feeding throughout the year to support the active growth and flowering periods. Like other orchids, they require high nitrogenous fertilizer in the spring to give an added boost to new growth and a general feed in the summer followed by a bloom booster in the autumn, which will assist in hardening the plant and preparing it for winter.

Dendrobiums from warmer climates can flower throughout the year and repotting should be done as soon after flowering as possible. They can be also be used as decorative landscape plants in tropical and subtropical zones where they will quite quickly and happily establish themselves on a tree trunk in full sun. Compost mixtures should be free-draining so that the plants can be watered regularly with fresh water. If attached to a tree, rainfall will readily soak the plants and drain through the medium without holding any unwanted water.

In a green- or shade house the plants require as much light as they can get. Be sure to use a very solid pot, as Dendrobiums can easily be top heavy. Plastic pots with a crock will suffice, but clay pots are ideal because they have a heavy base. This type of Dendrobium will easily adapt to basket culture.

Dendrobium densiflorum.

MASDEVALLIA

Origin	Mexico; Brazil; Ecuador; Colombia; Peru
Min/max temps	10–24°C (50–75°F)
Flowers	Triangular and often hirsute; must be kept consistently damp and cool
Light	Prefer very low light (60–70% shade) light feeders
Feeding	Highly unusual and collectable
Pronunciation	maz–de–val–ee–a

Masdevallia mendozae 'Orange Mint' AM/RHS.

The genus Masdevallia is one of the most curious groups of miniature orchids. Some 350 species exist, distributed from Mexico through Brazil, Ecuador, Colombia and Peru, growing epiphytically in mist-shrouded forests at high altitudes. Masdevallias belong to the subtribe of *Pleurothallidinae*, and worldwide there are specialized groups devoted to these mighty midgets. Most often single-flowered, some have multiple flowers on the stem. Their colours vary enormously from dull hues to bright fluorescents. Little plants will quite easily

Masdevallia Kimballiana (*caudata* x *veitchiana*) 'L&R'.

Masdevallia coccinea var. *aurea*.

establish themselves into specimen plants that produce multitudes of flowering stems. The flowers vary from 3mm up to 15cm (6in), but most have a distinguishable triangular shape and tend to be hairy in appearance.

CULTIVATION

The plants produce single leaves and thrive on being damp and cool at all times. Without this the leaves can become marked. Sphagnum moss or composts that retain a high moisture content are suitable for Masdevallias. The plants are quite susceptible to viruses that are often passed on by poor housekeeping or sucking insects. Keeping insects at bay will help to keep Masdevallias healthy. When making divisions, always use clean, sterilized tools. These plants are light feeders and respond well to a regular but light-feeding programme throughout the year. *Masdevallia coccinea*, which naturally occurs in vibrant pink, purple, white and yellow is a plant worth owning.

DRACULAS

Until the 1970s, *Dracula* orchids were treated as Masdevallias. The flowers of the *Dracula* genus can be quite sinister in appearance: dark, hairy and mostly pendulous. The plants are genuinely cool-growing and will stress in warm or hot climates without some form of air conditioning or cooling.

Because flowers emerge from the base of the plant (often from the bottom of the pot), *Draculas* are well suited to plastic waterlily baskets or small wooden slatted or wire baskets and should be grown in sphagnum moss so that the flowers can emerge without hindrance. While the plants will grow easily in the damp sphagnum moss they also enjoy a breeze to keep the moss cool.

Masdevallia and Dracula will hybridize together – resulting intergeneric hybrids are known as *Dracuvallia*.

Dracula roezlii.

Dracula chimaera 'Dark'.

Dracula exasperata.

Dracula robledorum 'Tapestry'.

BRASSIA

Origin	Tropical zones at high altitudes in the Americas
Min/max temps	12–25°C (53–77°F)
Flowers	Year round, with bizarre flowers tha resemble spiders
Light	Prefers semi-shade (50% shade)
Feeding	Medium feeders
Pronunciation	bras–ee–a

Brassias belong to a rather bizarre genus that includes almost 30 species originating from tropical America. They are allied to the Odontoglossum and Oncidium groups with which they readily interbreed.

These curious-looking plants have the appearance of large spiders, hence their common name, spider orchid. Each flowering stem carries from six to twelve large, long-lasting flowers.

CULTIVATION
Brassias occur at high elevations in damp forests, which makes them great companions for the cool- and intermediate-growing orchids. Being forest dwellers, they must be in semi-shade, much like the Odontoglossum

Alliance. Humidity is also important in order to keep their bulbs plump. They like an open, friable (crumbly) potting mix of bark and perlite and regular feeds of fertilizer at half the recommended strength.

Brassias can make fine specimen plants – there is nothing quite like a well-grown Brassia with several inflorescences full of spidery flowers. The flowers of the different species vary from creamy whites to pastel greens and bronze yellows. Some have mahogany barring that adds to their unique beauty. When used for hybridization with Oncidiums and Odontoglossums, Brassias offer some warmth tolerance as well as passing on their characteristic elongated petals and sepals.

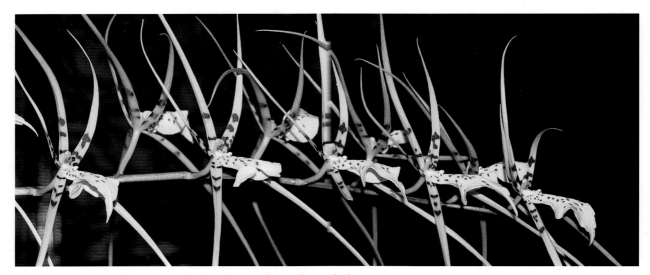

Brassia gireoudiana, also commonly known as a the spider orchid.

COELOGYNE

Origin	From India east to China and south to Indonesia and the southwest Pacific Islands
Min/max temps	12–25°C (53–77°F)
Flowers	Spring and early summer; basket culture recommended
Light	Prefers semi-shaded position (50% shade)
Feeding	Hungry feeders; very easy to grow
Pronunciation	soo–lod–gin–ee

Coelogynes are a fascinating group of orchids, many of which have showy flowers and delightful scents. They are easy to grow and quickly establish into large specimen plants. There are about 100 species in the genus Coelogyne, distributed in the highland areas of Asia, from India through China and south to Indonesia.

The plants have distinctive pseudobulbs and firm leathery leaves. The flowers range in colour from pure white to soft creamy hues and various shades of green. The more showy species are *Coelogyne pandurata*, which is bright green except for the lip which is marked with jet black. *Coelogyne cristata*, *C. dayana* and *C. flaccida* are great companions in any cool house.

CULTIVATION

Coelogynes are epiphytic by nature and will happily grow suspended from the greenhouse roof, where they can enjoy a bright, airy position. They thrive in semi-shade, and need to be protected from direct sunlight that might scorch their foliage.

Basket culture is recommended, as the plants do not like their roots being disturbed. When the specimen becomes too big for its basket, the whole basket can simply be placed inside a bigger basket without too much disturbance. The watering and feeding regimes for Coelogyne are similar to those of Cymbidiums (see pages 80–81).

Coelogyne cristata, one of the most popular of this species, is best suited to basket culture.

Orchids for intermediate climates

Intermediate orchids are those that grow in climates that are neither too hot nor too cool, but fall somewhere between the temperate and tropical zones. These orchids grow best in subtropical areas, where the temperatures rarely fall below 12–15°C (54–59°F) or rise above 24°C (75°F). Most orchids in this group prefer bright, although not direct, light and will be comfortable growing in a semi-shaded position such as a covered patio or verandah (40–50 per cent shade cloth).

OPPOSITE *Paphipedilum rothschildianum* 'Mont Millais' FCC/RHS/AOS.

ONCIDIUMS AND THEIR INTERGENERIC HYBRIDS

Origin	Distributed throughout the American tropics from Florida to Argentina
Min/max temps	15–30°C (59–86°F)
Flowers	Mostly autumn and winter
Light	High light
Feeding	Heavy feeders
Pronunciation	on–cid–ee–um

Oncidium species, their hybrids and intergeneric hybrids, are perfectly suited to intermediate and warmer climates. Oncidiums are one of the largest genera in the orchid family and there have been many botanic and taxanomic changes within this group, splitting the species into associated and related Oncidiinae genera. The plants are epiphytic by nature using hosts such as cactus plants and trees for support. They thrive in high light and enjoy regular watering in the dry hot summers in nature. Having pseudobulbs, Oncidiums will also respond to being regularly fed.

Oncidiums are closely related to Brassia, Miltonia, and Odontoglossum with which they will easily hybridize and add warmth tolerance to their hybrids. Aspasia and Cochlioda will also breed with Oncidiums. The intergeneric hybrids are easy to cultivate in intermediate conditions, they flower freely and they enjoy open compost mediums that do not hold too much water. The species and hybrids have white, needle-like roots that rot easily if saturated for too long.

In Europe especially, the most commonly cultivated hybrid must be Vuylstekeara Cambria 'Plush' and its variants. This plant is commonly known and grown by commercial growers such as Cambria – it is an intergeneric hybrid that was produced in England several decades ago. Modern hybridizing has introduced many new hybrids into the market and this group now accounts for a wide and varied group of orchid pot plants.

Oncidiums will grow and thrive in baskets, positioned in trees in a landscaped garden in a subtropical climate, or in pots in shade houses and controlled greenhouse environments.

Sadly the flowers of Oncidiums are often just yellow with brown markings, but once hybridized with Odontoglossum and Cochlioda they produce beautiful flowers in autumn tones, which often last in excess of six weeks.

Oncidium sphacelatum is well worth using in the garden in tropical or subtropical climates where the species will establish quickly in trees or hanging baskets. Hybrid Oncidiums to look out for are *Onc.* Sharry Baby that produces scents of chocolate, or *Onc.* Twinkle that offers a warm vanilla fragrance.

A tried and tested Oncidium extensively used as a commercial pot plant is Oncidium Gower Ramsey.

Water and Humidity

Oncidiums and their hybrids enjoy an open compost that holds moisture rather than water. A mix of bark and perlite suffices for pot culture, while slatted baskets can be filled with bark and a little chopped sphagnum moss. Oncidium species that enjoy a dry period will adapt to raft culture if they are tied to tree fern or cork slabs.

Oncidiums require frequent watering and buoyant air movement in order to dry off after watering. Humidity will discourage overly dehydrated pseudobulbs which need to be plumped up in order to produce often long stems of long-lasting flowers.

In a shade house or garden, more frequent mistings will reduce the chance of dehydration. Oncidiums are very varied in their growth, but generally a lime green colour to their leaves indicates a hardened plant that will probably flower better than a dark green one. Lack of humidity sometimes causes the leaves to be slightly crinkled, but this is easily overcome with additional spraying of water.

Temperature

The ideal temperature for most Oncidiums and their intergeneric hybrids is between a winter low of 15°C and a high of 30°C in summer. 30–50 per cent shade cloth is adequate as these orchids tolerate high light in most cases. Additional reading will dictate the exact requirements. Intergeneric hybrids that have Odontoglossum in their progeny will require additional shading.

Feeding

The intergeneric hybrids can tolerate regular feeds at half the recommended strength of most fertilizers once a week. A high nitrogenous feed in spring will encourage new growth and a balanced fertilizer in summer and winter will keep the plant at its peak. A high potash-based fertilizer in autumn encourages new flowering stems from the plump bulbs.

This genus and its hybrids will always flower better if the flowers are produced in winter or early spring. If a plant is ailing, it may be necessary to remove an emerging spike in the summer in order to save it.

Pests

Not many pests attack Oncidiums, though aphids will easily find flowering stems in an open shadehouse in the summer months when they are more prevalent.

Burrageara Ash Trees (*Charlesworthara* Campari x *Oda.* Shelley). A new Oncidium intergeneric hybrid.

TOLUMNIAS

Tolumnias were known as Equitant Oncidiums and are best grown as epiphytes on rafts of cork, or in small terracotta pots with tree fern fibre or osmunda. Although they love to be watered they must dry off completely between waterings, as they do not tolerate water at their roots. Tolumnias have short, squat xerophytic leaves but throw stems of up to 20 flowers of incredibly intense colour and bold markings, blotches or spots. It is easy to fall in love with these miniature orchids as they never fail to bring joy when they flower.

WARM-TOLERANT CYMBIDIUMS

Origin	Southeast Asia, Himalayas, China, Japan; Philippines to New Guinea; Northern Australia
Min/max temps	12–30°C (54–86°F)
Flowers	Late summer in a variety of forms and colours
Light	Provide good light, but no direct sun (30–40% shading)
Feeding	Hungry feeders
Pronunciation	sim–bid–ee–um

Cym. faberi, a species from China that has also been used in warm-tolerant Cymbidiums hybrids.

To keep in touch with collectors' needs, breeders began to produce a range of warm-tolerant Cymbidiums. Hybridists introduced *Cymbidium ensifolium* into their breeding programmes to ensure that flower buds would not drop in a tropical climate or during the European summer months. *C. ensifolium* is found naturally in China, Taiwan and the Philippines and is classified as a miniature because the flowers are considerably smaller than the standard and intermediate types. There are two colour forms, one being greeny-tan and the other a pure album (white). These offered hybridists opportunities to produce several colours, but *C. ensifolium*'s best characteristic is that it thrives and flowers in a warm climate with flowers normally borne in mid- to late summer. Other hybrids that were successful parent plants were *Cymbidium* Golden Elf and *C.* Peter Pan.

Cym. Golden Elf Tekweni 'Lemon Cream' AM/SAOC.

Cymbidium ensifolium and its hybrids made a huge impact on the market and there was further progress when the hybrids *C.* Sue, and the various forms and colours of *C.* Summer Pearl emerged. Newer hybrids include *Cymbidium* Mona Porters, *C.* Wild Colonial Boys, *C.* Florifame and *C.* Pretty Flamingo.

Hybrids have been made with other oriental warm-growing species such as *Cymbidium kanran*, but these have not been as successful as hybrids from *C. ensifolium* as the flowers tend to be too spaced out along the stem, and the segments are skinny compared with their shapely counterparts.

CULTIVATION

The plants are easy to grow and give great joy to those living in climates that are unsuitable for cool-growing Cymbidiums. Don't be disturbed by the black streaking that may appear on the leaves; much like Zygopetalums, which are also liable to get these markings, it is not a virus but a condition known as 'ticking' and the condition is usually caused by excessive heat. For warmth-tolerant Cymbidiums one should follow the same cultivation regime as for their cooler growing relatives (see pages 80–81).

Origin	Miltonia: Brazil, Ecuador, Colombia; Miltoniopsis: Colombia and Ecuador
Min/max temps	Miltonia: 15–30°C (59–86°F); Miltoniopsis: 14–24°C (58–75°F)
Flowers	Miltonia: Usually spring/late spring; Miltoniopsis: throughout the year
Light	Miltonia: Good light, no direct sun (30% shade cloth); Miltoniopsis: semi-shade (50%)
Feeding	Miltonia: Hungry feeders, raft or slab culture; Miltoniopsis: heavy feeders; easy to grow
Pronunciation	mil–ton–ee–ah; mil–ton–ee–op–sis

Miltoniopsis Robert Strauss 'Stonehurst' AM/RHS (*Augusta* x *Gattonense*).

Miltonias can be split into two groups: cool-growing Andean varieties known as Miltoniopsis, and warmer types that belong to the Brazilian family named Miltonia.

Miltonia spectabilis, the type specimen for the genus Miltonia, was imported from eastern Brazil as far back as 1837 when it was first named. *Miltoniopsis roezlii* and *M. vexillaria* were later introductions, imported from Ecuador and Colombia towards the end of the 19th century. Miltonias and Miltoniopsis are closely allied to Oncidium and Odontoglossum and there are several intergeneric hybrids between the related genera.

CULTIVATION OF COOLER-GROWING MILTONIOPSIS

Miltoniopsis have elegant arching sprays of flowers that bloom throughout the year but especially in the late spring. The flowers have full, rounded blooms with the appearance of a large velvety pansy, hence the common name pansy orchid. The flowers possess a soft rose fragrance that is also found in many of the hybrids now widely grown as pot plants. The foliage is bluish-grey.

Unlike the warmer growing Miltonias, Miltoniopsis prefer pot culture and semi-shaded conditions. Their foliage is a bluish grey colour and they definitely thrive in a slightly cooler climate to their Brazilian cousins. Miltoniopsis are not difficult to cultivate, given a few specific conditions.

Water and humidity

These orchids should be potted in a well-drained mix of bark and perlite, or bark and coconut chips to allow for a free flow of water. They enjoy frequent watering, but

Miltoniopsis Orkney 'Starburst' (*Jules Hye de Crom* x *Colwell*).

compost must be allowed to dry just to the point of dampness before the plants are watered again. With good air movement in the greenhouse, watering would usually be required every other day in the summer and possibly only once or twice a week in the winter. In a shade house, however, more regular watering is required as it is likely that the growing media will dry out more quickly and there will also be less humidity in the air.

Humidity is vital for Miltoniopsis. A sure sign of inadequate humidity is the crinkled look of new leaves. To prevent dehydration, damp down the shade house floors and mist the plants on a regular basis. In an enclosed greenhouse the humidity is more easily controlled.

Temperature

The ideal temperature range for Miltoniopsis is between 14°C (58°F) and not much over 24°C (75°F). In the summer, at least, a 50 per cent shade cloth will be required for the Miltoniopsis as they cannot tolerate too-high light levels and the beautiful foliage is easily scorched.

Feeding

Treated much like the Odontoglossums, Miltoniopsis are fairly heavy feeders. After being repotted in the spring they require a regular feed of 30:10:10 high nitrogen-based fertilizers to encourage a spurt of new root and foliage growth. The fertilizer must be changed in summer to an 18:18:18 general feed that will plump up the bulbs and give the plant enough sustenance to see it through the autumn. At this point, the plants should receive a high potash-based bloom booster that will initiate the production of flowering stems.

Pests

Red spider mites may attack, and thrips can damage the buds on emerging flowers, but both of these are unlikely if the right conditions are given, and both are easily dealt with.

Miltonia spectabilis var. *rosea* is a warm-growing specimen that will easily grow into a specimen plant.

CULTIVATION OF WARMER-GROWING MILTONIA

Brazilian Miltonias have lush, lime-green, somewhat elongated foliage and tend to have a rhizome between each new bulb. Like Miltoniopsis, they grow easily in pots, on a cork raft or in slatted wooded baskets.

Miltonias will not tolerate being too wet. Although they love humidity and regular watering, they require good air movement to dry the plant soon after a shower. Miltonias do well in a warm, bright climate or a sunny position in the greenhouse.

Warmer types usually have one to two flowers on a stem but can easily be grown into large specimen plants and will produce several inflorescences. These will all flower at the same time and create a mass of colour.

Slab or raft culture

Brazilian Miltonias are best suited to culture in baskets. Slatted Vanda-type baskets can be filled with fairly coarse bark and chopped sphagnum moss to help retain moisture, or the plants can be attached to a cork raft on a small pillow of sphagnum moss, so that they become attached to the raft more quickly.

Miltonias do not like to be separated or split into smaller divisions and have been known to sulk for some time after being divided. If the division is too small, they may visibly deteriorate, or even perish altogether. They do not like to be repotted regularly either, hence raft culture is excellent as it does not require frequent maintenance or handling. Firmly secure the plant to the raft by carefully stapling it to the cork or tying it using old nylon pantihose (stockings). By the time the plant is properly attached and thriving on the raft the staple will have rusted and disintegrated, or the nylon perished, and both can be removed easily. Miltonias can stay on the same raft for several years without being disturbed. Basket-grown plants can easily be transferred to a larger basket when necessary without causing the plant undue stress.

Water, light and feeding

Although Miltonias enjoy frequent watering and thrive in high humidity, they cannot tolerate having 'wet feet'. Water left at their roots overnight will stress the plant and cause it to rot.

Air movement, like water, is vital to ensure good health; a fan in the greenhouse will create buoyant air and assist in keeping Miltonias dry.

They like some shade in the middle of the day but also adore a brightly lit hanging position where they can enjoy a breeze.

The feeding regime for Miltonias is exactly the same as for Miltoniopsis kept under the correct conditions, Miltonias suffer from few, if any, ailments or pests.

OPPOSITE *Miltoniopsis* (Charlesworthii x Colwell).

PAPHIOPEDILUM

Origin	Tropical Asia, extending to India, China and Solomon Islands
Min/max temps	14–28°C (57–82°F)
Flowers	Autumn through spring, with some summer flowering varieties
Light	Provide dappled light (50% shade cloth)
Feeding	Light feeders; easy to grow, but free-draining compost is essential
Pronunciation	paf–ee–oh–ped–ee–lum

Maudiae group: *Paph*. Silver Fleuret 'Rockdale's Michael' AM/AOS (Gael x Holdenii).

Paphiopedilums, or slipper orchids, are one of the most curious orchid species. They belong to the family *Cypripedium* that include the genera *Phragmipedium* from Central and South America, *Selenipedium* from Central and South America and the true *Cypripedium*, extending from North America to Europe and Asia.

The lip of slipper orchids has evolved into a marvellously sculptured pouch that has the appearance of a shoe or slipper, hence the common name, lady's slipper. The pouches differ somewhat between each subtribe within the family.

Paphiopedilums are tropical and are naturally found in Asia, from India in the west over to China in the east and as far south as the Solomon Islands in the Pacific.

These primitive orchids have a huge following; Paphiopedilums were one of the first orchid groups to be

Paph. haynauldianum var. *album*, a rare albanistic form of this multifloral species.

the subject of specialized clubs that are now thriving on every continent. Members meet regularly to discuss new breeding trends, species and cultivation techniques, and disseminate knowledge throughout the world.

The first registered orchid hybrid was a Paphiopedilum. In 1869 the English nursery, James Veitch & Sons, registered *Paphiopedilum* Harrisianum (*P. villosum* x *P. barbatum*) and by 1900 they had produced another 470 hybrids.

The plants are evergreen and mainly terrestrial, but there are a few species that are naturally epiphytic. In the jungle they thrive in well-drained crevices, in humus, or on limestone cliffs, often overhanging deep gorges. In all cases, the plants are in shade for most of the day. Their leaves, which are reasonably fleshy, vary from shades of green through to beautiful patterns of grey and green mottling. The fleshy substance of the leaves makes up for the fact that Paphiopedilums do not

have pseudobulbs, or any store of sustenance, other than that stored in their leaves. Flowers emerge from the centre of the mature plant's axel and, depending on the plant, there may be just one, or many, flowers. There are approximately 80 species, with flowers ranging in colour from pure whites through to pretty pinks, vinicolour reds, greens, purples, yellows, oranges and browns. Flowers emerge from the centre of the mature plant's axle; depending on the plant, there may be just one, or many. The shape of the flower varies as much as the colours do.

Over the years new Paphiopedilum species have been discovered, most recently in Vietnam, but these are protected by CITES and therefore prohibited entry to any of the world's hybridizing programmes.

Paphiopedilums can be divided by subgenus into many different groups, some of which are described on the following pages.

Maudiae group: *Paph.* Via Quatal 'Jamboree Emerald' HCC/AOS (*Via Quatal* x *Via Quatal*), a sibling cross using two seedlings of the same hybrid.

MAUDIAE GROUP

The mottled leaf, or Maudiae group, is possibly the very easiest to cultivate. Their patterned leaves make these very attractive plants even when they are not in flower. They can mature quickly into specimen plants, often giving several flowers with good lasting qualities even after only a few years. *Paphiopedilum callosum* and *P. lawrenceanum* are among the most popular. The most famous hybrids are *Paphiopedilum* Maudiae, *P.* Goultenianum and *P.* Claire de Lune.

Flowers range in colour from the most commonly occurring pink-rose with a striped dorsal to the album form (striking green and white), and the vinicolour form (those that naturally occur in deep burgundy reds almost verging on black).

COCHLOPETALUM GROUP

Equally impressive is the Cochlopetalum group, which contains the successive flowering varieties (on a mature plant for over 12 months). Each flower will last up to four weeks before falling, and is followed by another further up the stem – the process continues to the end of the stem. This characteristic is passed onto the progeny with remarkable success.

The flowers all have similarities but vary in size and colour, most noticeably in the species *Paphiopedilum glaucophyllum*, *P. primulinum*, *P. primulinum* var. *purpurascens* and *P. chamberlainianum* and its varieties.

A number of very impressive, majestic hybrids with multifloral species have been produced by breeding plants in the *Cochlopetalum* group, namely *Paphiopedilum* Vanguard, *P.* Transvaal and *P.* Prime Child. Cochlopetalums have been less than successful in breeding with the Maudiae types, mostly because of their chromosomal incompatibilities.

Cochlopetalum group: *Paph.* St Swithin x *primulinum.*

Multifloral: *Paph. philippinense* var. *album.*

Paph. (*sanderianum* x *malipoense*), a hybrid between a multifloral and a Parvisepalum.

Multifloral: *Paph.* Mount Toro (*philippinense* x *stonei*).

Maudiae group: *Paph*. Sue Franz 'Willowdale' HCC/AOS (William Matthews x Cyberspace).

Parvisepalum group: *Paph*. Magic Lantern (*delenatii* x *micranthum*).

Parvisepalum group: *Paph. jackii* var. *album*.

Parvisepalum group: *Paph*. Fanaticum (*micranthum* x *malipoense*).

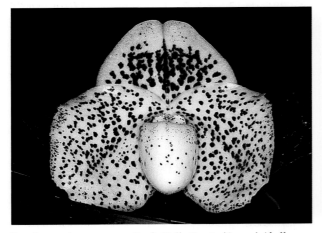

Brachypetalum group: *Paph*. Bella Lucia 'Super' (*bellatulum* x Wellesleyanum)

Green leaf group: *Paph*. (Keyeshill x Luther Pass) 'Ruby Glow'.

MULTIFLORALS

The most regal of all Paphiopedilums are surely the multifloral flowering species and their hybrids, not only when they are crossed in the same group, but also with others. Species in this group are referred to as strap-leafed Paphiopedilums because their dark, lime-green coloured leaves are rigid and firm. Of all the slipper orchids, these take longest to mature, and plants grown from seed can take from eight to ten years to flower for the first time. Hence, the orchids in this group command a higher price than most. The majestic *Paphiopedilum rothschildianum* must rate as the king of orchids, closely followed in magnificence by *P. sanderianum* with its long trailing petals, which can reach up to 60cm (24in) or more. *Paphiopedilum stonei*, *P. philippinense*, and *P. lowii* are also outstanding examples.

Noteworthy hybrids are *Paphiopedilum* Prince Edward of York, a hybrid made in the early 1900s but lost to cultivation during the two World Wars. It has since been remade after *P. sanderianum* was rediscovered in Borneo in the mid 1980s. *P.* Michael Koopowitz, *P.* Saint Swithins and *P.* Lady Isobel are easy to cultivate and flower readily once mature

BRACHYPETALUMS

Brachypetalums are the most difficult to grow of all the Paphiopedilums in that they prefer drier conditions than the others – many are sacrificed by over-watering. They love fresh air movement, enjoy being showered, albeit infrequently, and thrive in high humidity.

They have short stems, but incredibly beautiful flowers that are usually fuller and rounder than most other Paphiopedilums. The plants have slightly mottled foliage; their succulent leaves have a crystalline finish that glistens and sparkles on well-grown plants.

The species in its own right is very bold, and breeding from it with other groups can be difficult and problematic. The short stem is unfortunately a bad characteristic that is passed on to immediate progeny. *Paphiopedilum bellatulum*, which features probably more than any of the other species within this group, can be quite variable, but is distinguished by its bold maroon spotting. *Paphiopedilum niveum*, *P. concolor*,

and *P. leucochilum* are significant in this group. Album forms of these species are very dominant in the production of white complex *Paphiopedilums*, which have proved quite elusive.

GREEN-LEAF SPECIES

The green-leaf species, which includes *Paphiopedilum fairrieanum*, *P. exul*, *P. villosum*, *P. insigne* and its colour forms, and *P. charlesworthii*, nearly all originate from India and farther east. The plants are normally robust and require only simple cultivation methods to grow well. They grow readily, and soon establish themselves as specimen plants with long-lasting flowers. This group can also tolerate the cooler winter temperatures which encourage flowering.

The green-leaf group encompasses all the large flowered hybrids, and the species makes up a big part of their lineage with lesser insertions of Brachypetalums. It is the large complex hybrids that produce huge, showy single blooms that have a plastic appearance and come in a vast array of colours, from pure shades to spotted white, green, yellow, red and brown. The large, flowered hybrids are often listed as Complex Hybrids or American Hybrids and are sadly often known as 'cabbages' because of their large, firm-textured flowers.

PARVISEPALUMS

The most recent Paphiopedilum introductions, species from China and Vietnam, form the subgenus Parvisepalum, which includes the bright yellow *Paphiopedilum armeniacum*, the bubblegum pink *P. micranthum*, apple-green *P. malipoense* and its ally *P. jackii*, as well as the rediscovered pink *P. delenatii*, cream *P. hangiaum* and the most recently discovered pink-purple *P. vietnamense*.

This group has produced several beautiful hybrids that have all passed on the dominant characteristic of a large bubblegum ball-like pouch. Many of the species are fragrant and in some cases this too has been passed to the progeny. Seedlings were somewhat difficult to grow at first, but once their cultivation was better understood the plants survived and, with few exceptions, grew as easily as other slipper orchids.

CULTIVATION

Evergreen and mainly terrestrial, a few species are naturally epiphytic. In the jungle, they thrive in humus, in well-drained crevices, or on limestone cliffs, often overhanging deep gorges. In all cases, the plants are in shade for most of the day. Leaves vary from shades of green through to beautiful patterns of grey and green mottling, and are reasonably fleshy because *Paphiopedilums* have neither pseudobulbs nor any other store of sustenance, other than that stored in their leaves.

Potting mix and repotting

Generally, slipper orchids are quite easy to grow given that they are planted in an open mix that can vary from bark, perlite, sphagnum moss, tree fern fibre or osmunda, limestone gravel, expanded clay balls or even nut shells; in fact, almost any mix that is friable. In cooler climates a bark and perlite mix is adequate, but in warmer climates, where the plants are grown in shade houses or outdoors in an uncontrolled environment and may get watered by rain, it is vital to use a mix that does not hold too much moisture.

Paph. bellatulum var. *album.*

Normally, slipper orchids flower from autumn to spring but some varieties will also flower in the summer. It is important to repot as soon as possible after flowering. A Paphiopedilum in poor condition can be repotted at any time as this will often push the plant into producing new roots and growth.

Water

In nature, Paphiopedilums are used to regular watering, especially in summer monsoon climates where they enjoy thorough downpours most afternoons. While the plants enjoy lots of fresh water, they do not like to stand in it. Paphiopedilums grow naturally in free-draining places such as rock crevices or on the face of limestone cliffs, where they receive much rain but can quickly dry off due to the good air movement. The roots will rot easily if they stand in water, so if the plant is grown indoors stand it on a draining board after watering so that excess water can run off. It is best to water all orchids early in the day to give the plants time to dry out during the higher daytime temperatures. This is important, as water held overnight in the crown of the plant can lead to bacterial or fungal rots, which may eventually kill it.

Paph. concolor 'Hill Tribe'.

Paph. Kabuki Moon (Virgo x *emmersonii*) is a hybrid between the Bracypetalum and Parvisepalum groups.

Light
Slipper orchids love dappled light, whether it be in the home, the greenhouse, or in their natural environment. Their leaves can scorch with excessive light.

Feeding
Paphiopedilums do not possess pseudobulbs or any storage tank in which to hold reserves, so regular application of a weak fertilizer is recommended, but they are not heavy feeders.

Pests and diseases
Many Paphiopedilums succumb to *Erwinia*, a bacterial disease that is easily noticed as a brown rot in the growing apex of the plant. If this rot is observed, move the plant to a drier space and avoid overhead watering until the rot has been cured. There are few pests that attack slipper orchids, but mealy bug or woolly aphid can easily infest the leaf crevices and may be observed in the leaf axels or on the underside of the leaves. If you discover brown fungal or bacterial rot, especially on the green-leaf multifloral types, do not hesitate to move the plant to a slightly drier position and liberally sprinkle the leaves with cinnamon powder. The medicinal qualities of cinnamon are not really known, but it does work and, hopefully, will save the plant.

Propagation
Slipper orchids can only be raised from seed or by division if the plant is large. These orchids have not been successfully multiplied by tissue culture or cloning, hence collectors will pay high prices for prized Paphiopedilums. The plants are not difficult to raise from seed but can be slower than many other orchids to germinate. They require quite specific light conditions in the laboratory.

LYCASTE AND ANGULOA

Origin	Originally from South and Central America
Min/max temps	8–30°C (50–75°F)
Flowers	From late autumn through early summer *Lycaste* may be scented sweet or spicy; Anguloas also have a scent
Light	Provide semi-shade, no direct sun (50% shade cloth)
Feeding	Heavy feeders
Pronunciation	*Lie–cas–tee*; *Ang–you–loa*

Lycaste (*cruenta* x Mem. Bill Congleton) 'Simon's Gold'.

Lycastes belong to the subtribe Lycastinae, which includes the genera Anguloa and Bifrenaria. More recently the genus Lycaste was split and a new genus, *Ida*, was described, which encompasses most of the green-flowered species. To avoid confusion and for the purposes of simplicity, the name Lycaste will be retained in this book. There are some 45 species in total in the genus, which can be found as far north as Mexico and as far south as Peru. The most well known is *Lycaste skinneri* from Guatemala, the country's national flower. It is currently listed as a Red Data (endangered) species and noted in CITES Appendix 1, making commercial trade in it illegal. Pre-CITES, many of these beautiful plants were exported from South America and have been widely grown and cultivated by all lovers of this exceptional genus.

The name Lycaste appears in the Greek classics, where it is associated with the colour white or silver. Hence, when the type specimen was described, a white *Lycaste skinneri* (syn. *Lycaste virginalis*) was illustrated. The species does, however, occur in various colours, from stark white to rose pinks and even blood red.

Flowers are almost triangular in shape with three prominent sepals. Blooms are mostly fragrant: *Lycaste skinneri* has a rich rose perfume, while some of the smaller deciduous species, like *Lycaste cruenta,* exude a spicy scent. Many hybrids are available in a range of colours and most are impressively floriferous, but these have lost favour as the plants can become too large for the average hobbyist's greenhouse.

Anguloas used to be cultivated as Lycastes. They are commonly called tulip orchids, because they produce upright-cupped flowers on an erect stem. Anguloas occur in a wide range of colours, from white to the bright buttercup yellow of *A. clowesii* to the dark orangey hues of *A. ruckerii.*

Anguloas can easily be grown with Lycastes as they enjoy similar conditions and also hybridize together quite successfully. Since the flowers are quite easily bruised and damaged in transport, they are not popular as pot plants outside their home countries. Within their countries of origin however, Anguloas are often seen growing in window boxes and on patios.

CULTIVATION
Lycastes have been in cultivation for over 150 years and are still widely grown in Japan, Australasia, England and the USA, although the species of Lycaste and Anguloa originate from South and Central America.

Temperature and humidity
These orchids are cool to intermediate growers, thriving in cool dry winters and warm humid summers. The deciduous group, particularly, requires a dry resting period in the winter or the plants will rot and die. In winter, this group exhibits very sharp spines on the top of old pseudobulbs from where the leaves have fallen off.

Angulocaste Olympus (Angste. Apollo x Lyc. Sunrise)

Lyc. Macama 'Atlantis' (Sunrise x Koolena).

While the plants may experience occasional frost in nature, in cultivation it is preferable that winter temperatures do not fall much below 8°C (50°F). Heating is definitely required in northern hemisphere winters, but in milder climates where night temperatures fall within the recommended range and frost is uncommon it may not be necessary. Summer temperatures should remain below 30°C (75°F).

In a green- or shadehouse, regular misting under benches during the warm summer months will create the required humidity – without it the plants will stress and the bulbs shrivel. Lycastes and Anguloas are best protected from extreme temperatures.

Air, light and water

Air circulation is important for Lycastes and Anguloas, as these orchids are epiphytic by nature and need to dry off after watering. Good air circulation will also prevent heat build-up in summer.

While light is important, a 50 per cent shade cloth will prevent harsh sunlight from scorching new leaves. Too much shade will prevent successful flowering; the same will occur if the plants are bunched up or positioned too close together on the bench.

Flowering generally occurs from late autumn to early summer. The plants must be kept moist at this time, but avoid over-watering. Offer frequent misting rather than heavy showers. The plants must not be allowed to stand in water at any time. Being epiphytic, they like regular watering but must be allowed to dry almost completely before the next watering. Deciduous species must be dried off gradually when the leaves begin to turn yellow in autumn as they prepare for their winter rest period. Commence watering when new growths appear in the spring. Plants in shade houses will dry out more quickly than those in an enclosed environment, unless adequate ventilation is available between watering.

Feeding

Lycastes and Anguloas enjoy regular feeding as they have large bulbs and produce abundant foliage. High nitrogenous fertilizers can be given in the spring to encourage new growth, followed by a general 18:18:18 balanced feeding throughout summer. A high potash-based fertilizer in autumn will harden off the plants for winter and act as bloom booster. Lycastes and Anguloas do not have to be fed in winter in climates with poor or low light as they will be in rest. Fertilizing at this time may even be detrimental to the roots and result in burning. The leaves readily reveal problems at the roots, such as unhealthy growth or burning from excess fertilizer.

Potting mix

These orchids thrive in an open, friable, well-drained mix – chopped sphagnum and perlite in equal parts is recommended. Potting mixes of peat, perlite and bark can be used in warm climates where the plants are heavily fed, but decomposes easily. To some degree, the rate of decomposition depends on the quality and grade of the bark, but be aware that the plant might need to be repotted annually with fresh compost.

Pests

Because of their large, softish leaves, Lycastes and Anguloas are susceptible to infestations of red or false spider mites that usually appear as a silvery shadow on the underside of leaves. Infestations can be remedied using arachnicides as soon as they are noticed. Spray regularly and with care, especially under the leaves.

Scale insects congregate underneath the older bracts on the pseudobulbs; removing the bracts will reduce the likelihood of infestation.

BULBOPHYLLUM AND CIRRHOPETALUM

Origin	Widely dispersed in tropical and subtropical regions throughout the world
Min/max temps	15–30°C (59–86°F)
Flowers	Flowers often have a hinged lip and some emit foul smells
Light	Provide semi-shade (50% shade cloth)
Feeding	Medium feeders; require high humidity
Pronunciation	bulb-oh-file-um and sirro-pet-alum

These curious orchids come from diverse climate zones around the world. There are well over 1,200 species and, with a surge in popular interest, new hybrids have begun to emerge. Bulbophyllums, and their close relatives the Cirrhopetalums, have become highly sought-after and collectable, probably due to their bizarre flowers: they produce some of the nastiest odours in the floral kingdom. *Cirrhopetalum graveolens*, for example, emits a smell of rotting meat to lure fly pollinators.

The plants occur naturally with many different growth forms and habits, from miniature to large, but most have creeping rhizomes, and spectacular and intricately complex flowers ranging from tiny and obscure to quite large. One interesting feature, more dominant in some species than in others, is that the flowers have a hinged labellum. A good example is *Bulbophyllum lobbii*. Whether drawn by scent, colour or form, when a prospective pollinator lands on the lip, it is propelled back towards the flower column by a forceful swing, thereby ensuring successful pollination.

The plants generally mature quickly into specimen plants, although some are slower than others. The spectacular *Bulbophyllum phalaenopsis* (not to be confused with the genus Phalaenopsis to which it is not related), produces almost one metre (3ft) long, broad, succulent, grey-blue leaves which hang pendulously from plump golf ball-sized maroon bulbs at the base of the plant. They are rarely seen, but a mature flowering plant, with its maroon flowers and filigreed lips, is a sight to behold. The plant smells putrid when fully open.

Cirrhopetalum graveolens.

CULTIVATION

Bulbophyllums are best grown in intermediate to warm conditions and are ideally suited to basket culture, as they do not like to be disturbed. They don't like to be divided either, so simply place their basket into a bigger one with some new potting mix when required.

They enjoy semi-shade and high humidity, and do not need large amounts of water if humidity is adequate. Consistent dampness is far more important than regular drenchings. Regular feeding with a weak concentration of fertilizer is required. Good ventilation and constant air movement will keep the plants healthy.

Warm-climate orchids

Warm-growing orchids originate in the tropics, making them ever-needy of warm, humid conditions in summer and only slightly cooler winter temperatures. Humidity is by far the most important factor for these tropical plants. While many tropical orchid species are from the east, Central and South America also have many beautiful species. Phalaenopsis and Paphiopedilums have proved popular for hobbyists and hybridists, and these genera are now cultivated in their thousands as pot plants in Europe. Cattleyas and Phragmipediums from the Americas are increasingly popular, while tropical species from Africa are mainly grown only by specialized orchid collectors. Ideally, warm-climate orchids enjoy a minimum temperature of 15°C (59°F) and a maximum of 30°C (86°F).

OPPOSITE *Phragmipedium caudatum.*

PHALAENOPSIS (MOTH ORCHID)

Origin	Tropical, South, Southeast and East Asia
Min/max temps	15–30°C (58–90°F)
Flowers	Throughout the year, especially spring
Light	Provide bright light, but no direct sun (60% shade cloth)
Feeding	Easy to grow
Pronunciation	fal–a–nop–sis

Phalaenopsis stuartiana 'Grange Gold', AM/AOS.

Phalaenopsis were some of the first imported orchids. Victorian growers found them relatively simple to cultivate, but their successes were mostly due to luck: the misconception at the time was that all orchids enjoyed hot, steamy environments. As a result, many of the cool and intermediate species perished. The tropical Phalaenopsis, however, thrived in the hot, humid stove houses of the era. Phalaenopsis have adapted well to modern cultivation methods, so much so that they have become one of the most popular of houseplants in Europe.

Phalaenopsis is also known as moth orchid because when the *amabilis* species was first observed in its natural habitat, the long inflorescences of pendulous white flowers that festooned the jungle treetops were thought to be clusters of moths.

There are some 70 species in the family, ranging from large and stately plants to tiny miniatures that could fit into a matchbox. Flowers range from showy whites to pastel pinks, and some are perfumed.

Phalaenopsis originate from the jungles of South and Southeast Asia, Indonesia, Malaysia and the Philippines, where they are found high in the trees of the dense forests. Most are evergreen, but a few miniature deciduous species lose their leaves in winter. It was once thought that Phalaenopsis and other orchids were parasitic, but this is not true – orchids only use their host trees as a means of support and do not leech nutrients off them.

The leaves are quite succulent and are used as storage vessels as the plants have no bulbs. The attractive grey roots absorb moisture and nutrients from the leaf mould in the bark crevices, and the plants thrive in their warm, humid atmosphere where rain is common in the monsoon season, but infrequent or absent during the rest of the year. In their natural habitat the humidity remains high, and the temperature rarely drops much below 15°C (59°F) in the middle of winter. There is always a warm breeze to dry off any excess moisture after rain, ensuring that the plants do not retain water in the apex of the leaves, thereby preventing any bacteria or fungal rot.

There are some closely allied genera that will happily breed with Phalaenopsis, most notably Doritis, hence the intergeneric hybrid name Doritaenopsis (Doritis x Phalaenopsis). While some Doritaenopsis hybrids look exactly like Phalaenopsis, following just one insertion several generations back, and may have also lost the appearance of any Doritis, they are still known as Doritaenopsis.

CULTIVATION

The new Phalaenopsis hybrids are ideal as houseplants and are able to thrive happily in a normal household

Phalaenopsis Hilo Lip (Hilo Beauty x Elaine Mishima).

environment. This is considered to be a temperature range that does not fall much below 14°C (58°F) in winter – when the central heating is usually on – and rarely goes over 30°C (85°F) in summer.

When there is insufficient humidity the plants should be misted on a daily basis using a spray bottle. Plants usually only need to be watered with a large cup of water

Phalaenopsis Be-Tris (Be Glad x Equestris), a miniature hybrid showing distinctive peloria, where the lip has fused to the petals.

Phalaenopsis Brother Redland Spots 'Crownfox' HCC/AOS (Golden Peoker x Brother Fancy) – a clean and colourful new *Phalaenopsis* hybrid.

when the compost has nearly dried. This may be once or twice a week in summer and only once every two weeks in winter. If the plants have been used in a decorative arrangement, a few blocks of ice placed on the moss will ensure they are kept adequately watered. Never stand them in water, as this is a sure death sentence for Phalaenopsis, more of which are killed by over-watering than by any other means.

Potting mix

Phalaenopsis are epiphytic by nature but have adapted to become excellent pot plants. They will extend aerial roots once they are satisfied that there is enough support inside the pot. A very open mix of medium sized bark and perlite is recommended, or a mix of expanded clay, some sphagnum moss and tree-fern fibre. Any potting mix will eventually deteriorate and become sour – in this case the plant will also begin to extend aerial roots out of the pot.

Phalaenopsis should be repotted annually. In the Far East, only sphagnum moss is used for many orchids. This has proved very successful as it retains enough water and humidity, but in very warm climates algae can build up on the moss (detrimental unless the plants are repotted regularly, which can be both expensive and time-consuming).

Flowering

In nature, bud formation is induced by the drop in night temperatures; flowering commences in spring. Modern growing methods and the cooler temperatures prevalent in specialist greenhouses allow flowering all year round. In warm climates, where Phalaenopsis are mainly cultivated in shade houses, the plants may only flower in winter and spring. Phalaenopsis can be repotted at almost any time, but it should be avoided in winter in cold climates.

Mature plants usually carry four or five pairs of leaves. The flower stem emerges from between the leaves, looking like a root at first until its greenness and flat tip reveal a growing stem. Nodes form along the elongating inflorescence. The buds swell before the flowers open. It is vital to try and maintain as constant a temperature as possible, as a big drop can cause unopened buds to fall off before opening. A climate that is too dry will cause the young buds to dry and fall off, so it is also important to maintain humidity.

Insert a stake into the pot as close as possible to the stem and, as it elongates, train the stem and tie it lightly twice up to the first bud. The stem will naturally grow further and become pendant as the flowers begin to open. Branched stems may be tied past the first bud as the many flowers can become heavy when they open and the inflorescence can break. Avoid trussing the stem, as this can be unsightly. Flowers are long-lasting and Phalaenopsis have been known to be in flower for several months at a time.

Temperature, water and humidity

The ideal temperature range is 15–30°C (59–86°F). Phalaenopsis must be watered regularly, allowing the growing media to become almost dry before watering again. Indoors, water once or twice a week in summer, but only once every two weeks in winter. Overwatering can result in death. Humidity is important – the plants can survive without water, provided humidity is maintained. Humidity is easily achieved in a controlled greenhouse environment, but more difficult in an airy shade house. Plants kept here will need regular applications of water.

Lack of humidity and water will cause the leaves to become flaccid and it will be difficult to rehydrate the plant. Too much water, on the other hand, will cause fungal diseases and bacterial rots. For good health, the plants are best watered in the early morning so that excess water can evaporate before nightfall. In an enclosed greenhouse fans should be used to circulate the air, dry off surplus moisture and thus eliminate the chance of disease.

Light

Moth orchids will not tolerate high levels of light. Direct sunshine will scorch and mark the succulent fleshy leaves and leads to problems that prohibit the plant from properly transporting nutrients through the leaves. At least 60 per cent shade netting is necessary to reduce any chance of the plants being burnt or becoming stressed.

Phalaenopsis (Golden Poker x Sogo Manager).

Feeding

Phalaenopsis are not heavy feeders, but enjoy regular applications of fertilizer at half the recommended strength. High nitrogen-based feeds are best in spring, a general fertilizer throughout the summer, and a bloom booster in the autumn, returning to the general feed in the winter.

Pests and diseases

Phalaenopsis can become infested with mealy bug and scale insects, which must be dealt with as soon as they are noticed. Bacterial and fungal diseases can be detected by blackened blistering on the leaves, which permanently marks them and can be spread by water splashes. Isolate the infected plant, keep it drier than usual and avoid getting water on the leaves. Black honey mould (dull, black and mossy in appearance) can build up but can be wiped off using a damp cloth and some mild detergent.

Phalaenopsis can become stressed when they have been in flower and may indicate this by producing white streaks in the leaves. This can be remedied by removing the flowering stem and repotting the plant to give it a rest. Doritis species and hybrids can be treated in exactly the same way as Phalaenopsis. (See also the Vanda-Phalaenopsis intergeneric hybrid table, page 143.)

PHRAGMIPEDIUM

Origin	Tropical climates in South America
Min/max temps	15–30°C (58–90°F)
Flowers	Long-lasting; many species flower year-round
Light	Provide dappled shade (50% shade cloth)
Feeding	Light but regular feeders
Pronunciation	frag–mi–ped–ium

Phrag. besseae.

Phragmipediums are related to the tropical Asiatic slipper orchid (Paphiopedilum) and closely aligned to Cypripedium and Selenipedium. Endemic to South America, they are found in naturally boggy areas and damp crevices, or on rock faces in tropical climates that are typically warm and wet. First described in the late 1800s, the flowers of many species are quite bizarre, with long trailing petals that only stop lengthening when they touch the ground or display bench. The petals can grow to over 40cm (16in). Until the discovery of the red-coloured *Phragmipedium besseae* in the 1980s, the standard for flowers was shades of green and tan with some red pigmentation. The discovery of this new species created a frenzy of hybridizing activity among hobbyists hungry for new Phragmipediums, with the new plants claiming numerous quality awards. The remarkable red colour

Phrag. Les Landes (Grande x Hanne Popow) – a hybrid from *Phrag. schlimii* crossed with the long-petalled hybrid *Phragmipedium* Grande.

offered hybridists new challenges and many hybrids have inherited this enchanting characteristic. Phragmipediums have minimal light requirements and, unlike other orchids, like damp (they can be watered daily). Phragmipediums have made few intergeneric hybrids. Those made prior to the discovery of *Phragmipedium besseae* are divided into four main groups:

SHORTER-PETALLED GROUP
This group includes *Phragmipedium longifolium, P. sargentianum, P. lindleyanum* and *P. vittatum*. A good example is *Phragmipedium* Sorcerer's Apprentice.

LONG-PETALLED GROUP
Orchids in this group are bred from the species *Phragmipedium caudatum, P. wallisii* and *P. lindenii*, the latter being a rare example that does not have a sculptured pouch, but an extended third trailing petal.

Phragmipedium Grande, a famous, spectacular hybrid, falls into this group.

MINIATURE GREEN-FLOWERED
The green-flowered types, *Phragmipedium pearcei, P. hirtzii* and *P. ecuadorense*, possess short-stemmed grassy foliage and thin, twisted petals.

PHRAGMIPEDIUM SCHLIMII
There are many hybrids from this appealing, miniature, shell-pink species. All have inherited a pink colour and broad petals similar to *Phragmipedium* Schroderae. *Phragmipedium besseae* has been used with all the groups, with some amazing results: oranges and intense red hues have emerged with shapely, large flowers. There are also interesting prospects under development using the rare yellow or aureum form of *Phragmipedium besseae*. Like many orchids, *Phragmipedium besseae*

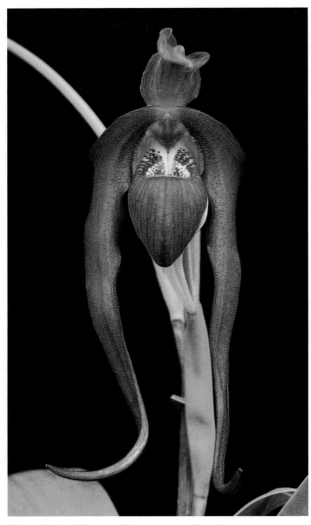

Phrag. Ruby Slippers (*besseae* x *caudatum*).

Temperature, water and humidity

Being from the tropics, the plants thrive in warm, damp conditions. Minimum winter temperature should never fall much below 15°C (60°F), as cold damp conditions will cause fungal and bacterial diseases. Warm, humid conditions in the summer are ideal.

Humidity can be created easily in a warm greenhouse by additional misting under the benches and even atmospheric misting during the warmest part of the day. Plants grown in shade houses can be watered on a daily basis in the summer and can even stand in shallow pans of water (which should not be allowed to become stagnant). Fresh water must drain through the media, ensuring that there is no algae build-up in the pans. Phragmipediums can be watered overhead as this will wash dust from the leaves and allow the leaves to transpire less if the humidity falls. Phragmipediums need good ventilation to ensure that any water in the growing apex can dry off, preventing waterborne bacterial rots such as Erwinia.

Light

Dappled shade is fine for Phragmipediums. They do not like too much light.

Potting mix and feeding

Calcium can be added to the mix in the form of powdered dolomitic lime, which will also neutralize any acidic peat-based composts that are used. Use a good open mix, anything from lava rock, sphagnum moss and tree-fern combinations to bark, perlite or water-absorbent rockwool with the addition of horticultural-grade foam to keep the rockwool from compacting.

Fertilize often using half of the recommended strength on most applications. A general fertilizer can be used year round, but a bloom booster in the autumn will prepare the plants to harden off for winter. Always repot when flowering is complete.

Pests and diseases

Few pests attack Phragmipediums. Fungal attacks and bacterial rots, due to over-watering or excess coldness and dampness, can be limited with good air circulation and temperature control.

has been closely observed and it has emerged that there are two distinct species. Plants with flowers that appear rounder and usually redder are the true *Phragmipedium besseae* from Peru. Those that are more orange in colour, with slightly swept-down petals, come from Ecuador and have been renamed *Phragmipedium dallesanderoi*. These tend to produce several branches on the stem, unlike their Peruvian cousin.

CULTIVATION

The hybrids are quick to mature and are easily cultivated if some simple guidelines are followed.

Phrag. China Dragon (*besseae* x Grande).

Shorter-petalled group: *Phrag.* Don Wimber 'Hayley Suzanne' AM/AOS (Eric Young x *besseae*), is an excellent form of this hybrid.

Phrag. Eric Young (*besseae* x *sargentianum*).

Phrag. Rosy Charm 'Suzanne' (Memoria Dick Clements x *schlimii*).

THE CATTLEYA ALLIANCE

Origin	Distributed throughout tropical Central and South America
Min/max temps	15–30°C (58–87°F)
Flowers	Appear annually and are long-lasting and fragrant
Light	Provide some shade, no direct sun (⟋% shade cloth)
Feeding	Heavy feeders
Pronunciation	cat-lee-a

With their large, pink, blousy flowers, Cattleyas are most people's archetypal idea of an orchid. Since Victorian times the spectacular blooms have been used for corsages and wedding bouquets. More recently they have become popular as houseplants. Flowers are long-lasting and, as an added bonus, possess a beautiful fragrance. Cattleya hybrids also produce the biggest orchid flowers.

Named in honour of William Cattley, a noted 19th-century English horticulturalist, this genus is extensive and the genus Cattleya falls into the subtribe Laeliinae, which encompasses many Cattleya-like species. Of the many intergeneric hybrids, Laelia, Sophronitis and Brassavola (now Rhyncolaelia) are the main genera used in hybridizing, but several other genera are compatible with Cattleyas and these are reflected in the intergeneric table (see page 136).

C. intermedia var. *orlata* 'Crownfox Jewel FCC/AOS.

Cattleyas may be specifically categorized by the growth habit of their leaves, which can be unifoliate (plants carry a single leaf on each pseudobulb), or bifoliate (plants carry two leaves on each growth).

There are about 50 species of Cattleya distributed throughout tropical America. They are characterized by an elongated pseudobulb carrying one or two firm, succulent leaves, and produce one or more flamboyant flowers, many highly fragrant. Flowers occur in a wide range of colours and vary in substance from velvety to waxy – many have a sparkling crystalline texture.

INTERGENERIC HYBRID PARTNERS

LAELIA

Some 60 species of Laelia occur from the West Indies into Mexico and south to Brazil. Flowers are varied and tend to be smaller than Cattleyas but are rarely single. In nature the plants grow in slightly cooler and drier spots than Cattleyas, but are very dependant on light.

BRASSAVOLA (RHYNCOLAELIA)

There are few species in the genus Brassavola (Rhyncolaelia) but these are no less spectacular, with the species *Brassavola digbyana* being the most beautiful in the family. Its prominent frilly lip, clear apple-green colour and greyish foliage has made it one of the most widely grown of all the Cattleya family. This genus can be found from Mexico to Honduras.

Laelia tenebrosa.

SOPHRONITIS

The Sophronitis genus has just seven species, all of them characterized by miniature growth and bright orange to deep red flowers. This genus was incorporated into hybridizing programmes to offer cool tolerance, and also to reduce the size of its progeny, making smaller, more manageable plants for a range of climates.

CULTIVATION

The Cattleya Alliance, or Laeliinae family, belongs to the intermediate to warm group of cultivated orchids. All these orchids thrive with high light, good late spring and summer watering and a reduction of water during the dormant winter rest period. Cattleyas can be cultivated in a range of situations: outdoors in trees in tropical landscaped gardens, as well as pot culture in shade houses and climate controlled greenhouses.

They are generally slow to mature, taking from three to four years to flower in ideal conditions. In Europe, where light levels are poor, especially in winter, plants can take as many as eight years to mature.

Cattleyas will flower annually, depending on the species used in the hybrids. In a relatively small collection of 20 or so plants, you should be able to enjoy flowers all year round. Buds are borne in a sheath at the top of the pseudobulbs, which open naturally as the buds emerge. The often large blooms will need to be supported in order for the beauty to be shown to its full potential; especially if the plant is to be exhibited at a show or in the home.

Light, temperature, water

Orchids in the Cattleya Alliance should be slightly shaded with no more than 40 per cent shade cloth. Even though they can tolerate higher light, they may become stressed and shrivel from excessively high temperatures. Ideal intermediate conditions range from a winter low of no less than 15°C (58°F) to a summer high of 30°C (87°F). In winter, the plants will stress if the temperature falls much below 15°C. It is vitally important that the plants are kept a little drier at this time. Extended exposure to cold, damp conditions will cause rot.

POPULAR CATTLEYA ALLIANCE INTERGENERIC HYBRIDS

Bishopara	(Bish.)	= Cattleya x Broughtonia x Sophronitis
Brassocattleya	(Bc.)	= Cattleya x Brassavola
Brassolaelia	(Bl.)	= Brassavola x Laelia
Brassolaeliocattleya	(Blc.)	= Cattleya x Brassavola x Laelia
Carmichaelara	(Crml.)	= Brassavola x Broughtonia x Laelia
Cattleytonia	(Ctna.)	= Cattleya x Broughtonia
Epicattleya	(Epc.)	= Cattleya x Epidendrum
Epilaeliocattleya	(Eplc.)	= Cattleya x Epidendrum x Laelia
Hartara	(Hart.)	= Broughtonia x Laelia x Sophronitis
Hasegawaara	(Hasgw.)	= Cattleya x Brassavola x Broughtonia x Laelia x Sophronitis
Hawkinsara	(Hknsa.)	= Cattleya x Broughtonia x Laelia x Sophronitis
Jewellara	(Jwa.)	= Broughtonia x Cattleya x Epidendrum x Laelia
Laeliocatonia	(Lctna.)	= Cattleya x Broughtonia x Laelia
Laeliocattleya	(Lc.)	= Cattleya x Laelia
Lowara	(Low.)	= Brassavola x Laelia x Sophronitis
Otaara	(Otr.)	= Cattleya x Laelia x Brassavola x Broughtonia
Potinara	(Pot.)	= Cattleya x Brassavola x Laelia x Sophronitis
Rolfeara	(Rolf.)	= Cattleya x Brassavola x Sophronitis
Rothara	(Roth.)	= Brassavola x Cattleya x Epidendrum x Laelia x Sophronitis
Sophrocattleya	(Sc.)	= Cattleya x Sophronitis
Sophrolaeliocattleya	(Slc.)	= Cattleya x Laelia x Sophronitis
Stellamizutaara	(Stlma.)	= Brassavola x Broughtonia x Cattleya
Stonia	(Sto.)	= Broughtonia x Sophronitis
Vaughnara	(Vnra.)	= Cattleya x Brassavola x Epidendrum
Yamadara	(Yam.)	= Brassavola x Cattleya x Epidendrum x Laelia

Winter rest

If the temperature drops below the ideal and the plants are dry, little damage will be done as long as they are not exposed to frost. In that case, they simply become dormant and will awaken when the weather has warmed up enough to stimulate new growth. Once plant and air temperature are sufficiently warm, it will take approximately two hours for the plant to begin functioning. Cattleyas should only be watered or fed when awake – they will be damaged if they are watered or fed when in sleep mode. During the summer months, the plants can be watered and fed earlier in the day. In summer, the plants require copious amounts of water to plump up the pseudobulbs and store nutrients for the winter dormancy.

Pests and disease

Excess humidity will cause fungus and bacterial infections that may lead to loss of new growth, or permanent spotting on the leaves.

Ants love the sugary substance produced by newly emerging flowers. They are carriers of scale insects, so be sure to remove old bracts and sheaths and groom the plants throughout the year. Viruses that infect the Cattleya Alliance are most visible when the plants are in flower and will show up as white striations on the flower. This condition is known as 'colour break' and the pale lines will soon turn to brown and mark the flowers.

Viruses are transferred from an infected plant by unsterilized cutting tools. Blades, secateurs and knives

Epic. Mae Bly 'Emy' HCC/AOS.

Propagation

Cattleyas can be divided when they become too big to handle. It is essential to use sterilized, sharp blades to make clean cuts and always plan the division, leaving at least three pseudobulbs per division. If divisions have good roots, 'pot on' in the usual way, using a pot that will only allow one to two years growth.

Because their long pseudobulbs tend to make Cattleyas top heavy, it is necessary to support them with a bamboo cane or wire support. If divisions are not supported, the plant will move around and this will damage any new and emerging root growth.

If Cattleyas have been neglected, quite often the older pseudobulbs (which may be leafless or even rootless) can be removed to encourage new growth. Like Cymbidiums, they can be put into a plastic bag and suspended under the bench. In time, the 'eyes' will develop and new growths begin to emerge, at which point the plant can be potted up in the normal way.

must be heated in a flame or sterilized using proprietary solutions to prevent the spread of viruses and diseases.

Potting mix and repotting

Cattleyas love very open, friable mixes that can be made with bark, coconut chips and osmunda, or bark and perlite. Granite chips lend weight for plastic pots.

Clay pots are ideal for a heavy plant but they dry out quicker than plastic pots, can be heavy to move and usually have to be broken in order to repot.

Pot on (see pages 52–55) annually when the plant is young or in its active growth period. Once it has matured and begun to flower, the plant only requires repotting every alternate year, as some mature plants can sulk if their root ball is interfered with.

The best time to repot the plant is soon after flowering, when the new growth appears at the base of old pseudobulbs, but before any new roots have begun to emerge. There is no doubt that repotting actively healthy plants stimulates new growth.

Feeding

Cattleyas are heavy feeders, especially during their very active growth cycle in spring. A high nitrogenous fertilizer used in spring may be changed to a general feed in the summer months, followed by a good-quality bloom booster that will harden the plant off and prepare it for flowering the following year.

CATASETUM

Origin	Warm climates from the West Indies, Mexico, Central and South America
Min/max temps	15–28°C (60–82°F)
Flowers	Flowers are produced in summer and are heterosexual
Light	Provide moderate light, no direct sun (50% shade cloth)
Feeding	Heavy feeders
Pronunciation	cat–a–see–tum

The family Catasetum offers flowers that can be quite bizarre in shape and colour. The flowers emerge from the base of a mature pseudobulb that carries soft green leaves and can vary from pure white to a deep red that appears almost jet black. Flowers can be narrow and simple, or broad and complex with heavily filigreed lips.

While most orchids are bisexual, this family can produce either male or female flowers. Both are fertile but are not both necessary to successfully pollinate a flower. Male flowers are generally more colourful and often display a trigger mechanism that ejects pollen with some force onto a possible pollinator's back. In this way, the pollen can be carried off to impregnate other flowers in close proximity.

Catasetums occur in the West Indies, Mexico, Central and South America, as far south as Argentina. There are some 70 species in this family that are closely related to Cycnoches, Clowesia and Dressleria. While this group of orchids does not make perfect houseplants, they are great greenhouse companions to Cattleyas, Paphiopedilums and Phalaenopsis.

CULTIVATION

Catasetums all require similar growing conditions. They are not difficult to cultivate at all, if simple instructions and guidelines are followed.

Temperature and light

Because of their origins, Catasetums prefer a warmer climate if grown outdoors but will also thrive in a controlled greenhouse setting. They enjoy warm temperatures with a minimum of 15°C (60°F) and a maximum of 28°C (82°F). Higher daytime temperatures will be tolerated if there is adequate humidity.

The plants are good companions to mottled-leaf Paphiopedilums and Phalaenopsis, enjoying moderate light and enough shading to prevent scorching of the soft, slightly plicate leaves.

Air and water

Good air movement is vital to prevent pooling of water in the new growths at the base of old pseudobulbs.

Catasetum pileatum.

Buoyant air will also keep the leaves healthy and avoid bacterial or fungal infections. Keep the plants dry during their dormant midwinter stage, as over-watering at this time can cause the roots to rot, which may prove fatal. Rot will also mean it may take much longer for the plant to re-establish itself in the spring, thus delaying flowering. The plants need copious amounts of water in spring and summer once the bulbs have begun to develop and the risk of cold weather has passed.

Much water throughout summer is necessary to keep the bulbs swollen and able to carry enough sustenance for winter.

Feeding

With the water, Catasetums require regular feeds with a high nitrogen-based fertiliser in spring to encourage the new growth, followed in summer by a general 18-18-18 fertilizer. To counteract the higher amounts of nitrogen in spring and summer, the plants will require a bloom booster in autumn to encourage flowering. As winter approaches, watering should be reduced – but always ensure that there is some moisture at the roots.

Potting mix and repotting

The orchids in this group are all epiphytes and thus require an open, well-drained compost of equal parts bark and perlite. This mix will hold some moisture, but in the warmest months watering will have to be done daily. In a controlled climate, moisture is easier to maintain; outdoors in a shade house where there is very buoyant air some chopped sphagnum moss could be added to help keep the mixture moist.

The plants will easily adapt to being grown on trees in a tropical garden. A cushion of sphagnum moss between the plant and the trunk will encourage new roots to emerge and adhere.

Repotting must be done annually. If the roots are healthy and in a good firm ball, the plant merely needs to be placed in a slightly bigger pot rather than disturbing the root ball. Rotten, soggy brown roots that may have been attacked by fungal infection should be removed: simply unravel the ball, remove any dead or damaged roots and pot into fresh compost.

On a mature plant, the oldest firm pseudobulbs can be removed. Although they may not have any roots, they

Catasetum tenebrosum.

should be potted into clean river sand or sphagnum moss until new growth appears, at which point the bulb can be potted up as usual. Take care to support the bulb so that the roots can establish without movement. The old back-bulb can also be potted into moss to encourage a new growth; alternatively, as with Cymbidium back-bulbs, it can be put into a clear plastic bag with the ends tied and suspended under a bench. After a relatively short period a new growth will emerge and the bulb can be potted up again, taking care to provide support for the growing plant.

Pests and diseases

There are few pests and diseases that affect Catasetums, worst of all being fungal and bacterial diseases relating to water left to pool and stagnate in the new growths.

Red and false spider mites may attack the soft leaves, creating a silvery lining on the underside, but a simple treatment of an arachnicide will usually deal with the problem.

VANDA AND ASCOCENDA

Origin	Same as Phalaenopsis, but also in Malaysia, Thailand, Borneo and Philippines
Min/max temps	10–32°C (35–98°F)
Flowers	Flowers are long lasting and produced annually
Light	Provide very bright light (20–30% shade cloth)
Feeding	Heavy feeders
Pronunciation	van–dah; asco–sen–dah

Ascda. Ken Kone 'Crownfox Sunglow' AM/AOS (*V. merrillii* x *Ascda.* Guo Chia Long).

Vandas and Ascocendas, like Phalaenopsis, are totally tropical orchids. The two families are closely related and occur in the same parts of the world, except that Vandas and Ascocendas can be exposed to full sun.

Malaysia, Thailand, Borneo and the Philippines are home to these epiphytic orchids. Vandas grow very large in comparison with Phalaenopsis, and have long trailing roots that draw moisture and nutrients from the atmosphere.

Vanda sanderiana (now known as *Euanthe sanderiana)* is a spectacular orchid producing racemes of bright pink and maroon flowers that have incredibly long-lasting characteristics. It has been used in many high-quality hybrids and is best known for the hybrid *Vanda* Rothschildiana, which is a cross with the blue, cooler-growing species *Vanda coerulea*. This is possibly the most famous Vanda hybrid and has been reproduced hundreds of times, resulting in what must be the bluest of all

Vanda Crownfox Velvet 'Shamwari', AM/AOS (Fuchs Fuschia x *sanderiana*)

orchid flowers, with heavy, white contrasting tessellations. The flowers are saucer-sized, flat blooms with extremely heavy substance and a crystalline texture that glistens in the light.

Vandas will hybridize with several genera, including *Ascocentrum,* the miniature Vanda lookalikes that pass on this characteristic to their progeny, thus producing small plants that are easy to handle and offer erect multiflowered stems of long-lasting flowers in a rainbow of colours. Other important genera that freely hybridize with Vandas are Rhyncostylis, Aerides, Neofinetia, Renanthera and even Phalaenopsis.

These tropical orchids flower reluctantly in climates with less intense light. They are widely cultivated in Asia (especially Thailand, Singapore and Malaysia) and also in Florida (USA) where some of the foremost hybridizers are situated.

CULTIVATION
Vandas and Ascocendas are widely grown around the world. In the Netherlands, where they are cultivated in enclosed greenhouses and offered additional light from halogen lamps, they grow reasonably well and flower successfully. In Durban, on South Africa's east coast, the plants thrive happily, despite the subtropical winter being cooler than normal, so the plants do go dormant; however, they revive with gusto in the spring to produce some fine-quality Vanda flowers. Florida is a centre of Vanda hybridizing, with a climate well suited to the requirements of Vanda and their allied genera.

The plants are generally grown in simple tunnels to protect the flowers from the elements, but are often seen growing naturally in gardens, adorning trees and on rocky landscapes. Vandas are typically epiphytic, and are sympodial, meaning that they generally have a single growth stem. The leaves are leathery and lime green in colour. Secondary plants emerge from the base of the main plant, which can be separated as soon as roots have begun to sprout.

Temperature, humidity, water, light and air
Tropical orchids must have high humidity and warmth and enjoy frequent watering. They require high temperatures in summer and, while winter temperatures can

Vascostylis Crownfox Red Gem 'Mardi Gras', AM/AOS (*Rhy. gigantea* x *Ascda.* Red Gem). This hybrid shows the very best of the *Rhynchostylis* hybrids.

Feeding

Vandas and the allied genera are heavy feeders and enjoy regular feeds. Use a high nitrogenous fertilizer (30:10:10) in spring to overcome any winter dormancy, followed by a general fertilizer in summer and a good bloom booster in autumn. Feeding is not required in winter but can be given if the temperature stays warm enough. If the plants are dormant from excessively cool weather, feeding them will be a waste, as they will not be able to absorb any nutritients.

Pests and diseases

There are few pests that affect Vandas, but scale is the most common. This can be spotted by the appearance of small, brown, bubble-like scales attached to the leaves. Initially, a wipe of methylated spirit on a cotton bud will remove most of the scales that can be seen, followed by a back up systemic spray. Chemicals are the least recommended route to follow, but bad infestations can only be treated in this way.

drop, they will perish if they are exposed to frost or cold for long periods in the open. In cool areas, the plants will become dormant in winter. This is not detrimental and can even be advantageous, initiating flower stems that produce bigger and better flowers. The ideal temperature range for Vandas is between a winter low of 15°C (59°F) and a summer high of 32°C (98°F). They will tolerate lower or higher temperatures for short periods without any damage or stress, provided they are kept dryish.

Light is extremely important for Vandas; too much shade will make the plants soft and leggy. In cultivation, 20–30 per cent shade cloth is adequate, while having a covered roof will definitely protect the blooms from harsh wind and rain. Vandas love being watered. This can be done on a daily basis in slightly drier but warm climates; otherwise, regular watering is required where true tropical climates exist and humidity is always high.

The plants like to be cooled by a constant breeze, so air movement is vital. Stagnant air will encourage fungal and bacterial rots, so in very warm, damp climates regular spraying is required to prevent fungal diseases.

BASKET CULTURE

While many books recommend potting media for Vandas and Ascocendas, these air-loving plants are best cultivated in wooden slatted baskets without any media. From seedlings, the plants must be secured to the base of the basket with wire so they cannot move around; in no time at all the young plant will attach itself to the basket and produce several roots. As the plant matures and the flower stems emerge, it is a good idea to make a firm wire stake to support a heavy head of flowers and show the blooms at their best. Over time, the smaller baskets can be placed into bigger ones until the plants are too big to handle, at which point they can be cut back and replanted into baskets of a more manageable size.

The basket method of planting is recommended, as the plants have less chance of picking up fungal or bacterial ailments that might cause them to lose their lower leaves, creating what is termed the 'palm tree' effect. Grown without media in a good climate, Vandas will keep all their leaves and maintain their attractive appearance.

POPULAR VANDA/PHALAENOPSIS INTERGENERIC HYBRIDS

Ascocenda	(Ascda.)	= Vanda x Ascocentrum
Ascofinetia	(Ascf.)	= Ascocentrum x Neofinetia
Asconopsis	(Ascps.)	= Phalaenopsis x Ascocentrum
Christieara	(Chrta.)	= Vanda x Aerides x Ascocentrum
Darwinara	(Dar.)	= Vanda x Ascocentrum x Neofinetia x Rhyncostylis
Devereuxara	(Dvra.)	= Phalaenopsis x Ascocentrum x Vanda
Doritaenopsis	(Dtps.)	= Phalaenopsis x Doritis
Ernestara	(Entra.)	= Phalaenopsis x Renanthera x Vandopsis
Kagawara	(Kgw.)	= Vanda x Ascocentrum x Renanthera
Mokara	(Mkra.)	= Vanda x Arachnis x Ascocentrum
Nakagawaara	(Nkgwa.)	= Phalaenopsis x Aerides x Doritis
Nakamotoara	(Nka.)	= Vanda x Ascocentrum x Neofinetia
Neostylis	(Neost.)	= Neofinetia x Rhyncostylis
Okaara	(Okr.)	= Vanda x Ascocentrum x Renanthera
Paulara	(Plra.)	= Vanda x Ascocentrum x Doritis x Phalaenopsis x Renanthera
Renanthopsis	(Rnthps.)	= Phalaenopsis x Renanthera
Rhynchovanda	(Rhv.)	= Rhyncostylis x Vanda
Sarconopsis	(Srnps.)	= Phalaenopsis x Sarcochilus
Vandaenopsis	(Vdnps.)	= Phalaenopsis x Vanda
Vandofinetia	(Vf.)	= Vanda x Neofinetia
Vascostylis	(Vasco.)	= Vanda x Ascocentrum x Rhyncostylis
Yonezawaara	(Yzwr.)	= Vanda x Neofinetia x Rhyncostylis

CULTIVATING MINIATURE SPECIES

Neofinetia falcata, the miniature Vanda relative from Japan and China, and its hybrids, can be cultivated in decorative oriental pots or bonsai dishes by mounting the plant on a tightly bound cushion of moss. To do this, form a small handful of moss into a ball. Place the plant on the ball, carefully wrap the roots around it and then bind them to the moss ball using light fishing line (be sure to use enough line to secure the plant properly). Push the ball firmly into the pot so that the plant sits proud. Water often enough to ensure that the moss ball is kept damp, but not wet, and fertilize as normal.

Miniature orchids make a very pleasing collection for growers who have limited home space, as they offer plenty of charming, colourful and often fragrant blooms. Some of the most spectacular orchids belong to the genus Angraecum, which is characterized by stark, glistening white flowers scented with hints of jasmine. Mostly night-scented, their sweet smell attracts moths from far and wide. The insects probe the depths of the flowers' spurs to drink the nectar and, as their probiscus is withdrawn, pollen is removed from the column and placed on the stigmatic surface of the flower, thereby ensuring pollination.

ANGRAECUM AND AERANGIS

Origin	Africa and Madagascar
Min/max temps	10–32°C (35–98°F)
Flowers	Flowers are usually white, night-scented and highly fragrant
Light	Provide very bright light (20–30% shade cloth)
Feeding	Medium feeders; water and feed regularly
Pronunciation	ann–gray–cum; air-ran-giss

Angraecums and Aerangis flower freely when well grown and also thrive when cultivated in greenhouses. Being epiphytic, these species enjoy similar treatment to Vandaceous orchids and will tolerate bright light, often in full sun, but will also adapt to a semi-shaded position.

Angraecums and Aerangis all like plenty of clean water at the roots; less so in winter than in the hotter months.

The bigger, stronger and more robust species are best grown in pots half filled with rocks, and the remainder of the potting media made up of some fresh sphagnum moss and chunks of large bark. The smaller members of the Angraecum family happily exist in teak baskets with some tree-fern fibre and sphagnum moss. Alternatively, they can also be firmly secured to a block of wood, with sphagnum moss packed around the roots for extra moisture (this should be done immediately after potting or mounting, in order to settle the plants).

Aerangis luteo alba var. *rhodosticta.*

Aerangis biloba.

CALANTHE

Origin	South and East Asia, the Malay Archipelago, the Philippines, New Guinea, SW Pacific Islands, east Australia, Madagascar, tropical and South Africa, Central America and the West Indies
Min/max temps	15–30°C (58–90°F)
Flowers	White, pink and red, long lasting
Light	Bright light
Feeding	Heavy feeders once new growths have developed
Pronunciation	cal–anne–thee

Known as Victorian or Christmas orchid, Calanthe was aptly named by early growers because it flowers profusely during December in the northern hemisphere. The red, pink, maroon and white flowers can last for up to a month. In the southern hemisphere, Calanthes flower in the winter months (Jul–Aug) and can be a useful asset to any orchid exhibit at that time.

CULTIVATION
Calanthes enjoy good humidity as well as good air movement.

Flowering
Once the flowers start to mature and buds form, the stems may need some support, which can be done with the aid of a thin cane and a single tie. When flowers begin to fade, the stems can be placed in a vase and the plants given a dry rest period. If the leafless pots are to be enjoyed indoors, a few maidenhair ferns will grace and complement these very Victorian orchids.

Repotting
Calanthes have large, conical bulbs that must be repotted annually for best results. After flowering the bulbs must be left to go dormant until early spring. Then remove them, shake off excess compost and snip dead roots with a sterilized cutting tool. It is important to use sterilized tools, as Calanthe orchids transmit viruses more readily than other species.

Calanthe St. Brelades (Corbiere x Saint Aubin).

Prepare a compost of bark and perlite, with the addition of some potting soil. If available, include some dried cow manure. (It must be old and dry already, as fresh manure carries too many pathogens and can encourage nematodes.) Place crocks in the bottom of the pot to ensure good drainage, then fill with dampened compost and press the prepared bulbs into it. Now water the plant lightly until the new growths emerge and are ±3cm (2in) high. From this point, they will require copious amounts of water and regular feeding.

Feeding

A high nitrogenous fertilizer in the spring will encourage good growth. A general 18:18:18 fertilizer throughout summer will mature the plant with its soft, plicate leaves.

As autumn approaches and the temperature starts to fall, the leaves will begin to turn yellow. By the end of autumn, they will have fallen from the plant. This is normal, so do not cut them off before they fall as some much-needed sustenance is returned to the bulb by the leaves before they fall. Avoid soggy compost at this stage, and continue to feed regularly until the plant becomes active again in the spring.

Pests and diseases

Calanthes are vulnerable to red spider mites, which can be dealt with by the application of a good arachnacide. Sadly, if it becomes infected by a virus, the only remedy is to destroy the entire plant.

Calanthe Grouville (Diana Broughton x Bryan).

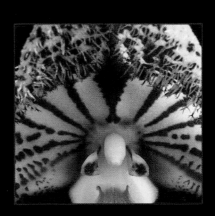

Further information

GLOSSARY

alba (albino, album) – flowers that lack any red pigment and are usually of pure yellow or white.

aerial roots – roots that usually emerge from the stem, above soil or medium level.

alliance – group of genera within a single tribe which share common characteristics and can be cross bred (produce a new hybrid genera).

apex – tip or growing point of a plant, usually a leaf or a shoot. (*See* crown)

axil – angle between the emerging leaves from where a bud will appear.

back bulb – often referred to as pseudobulb or pertaining to any old bulb without a leaf or leaves, especially those of Cymbidiums.

bract – may resemble a new leaf on a new growth but will form part of the covering on mature pseudobulbs.

capsule – referring to a seed pod.

chromosome – structure within a cell responsible for the hereditary characteristics or genes.

clone – group of genetically identical plants, which have been vegetatively propagated. (*See* meristem/mericlone)

concolour – flowers of one single colour, especially referring to albino flowers that have no red pigment.

crown – part of the plant from where new leaves are produced. (*See* apex)

cultivar – derived from 'cultivated variety'. An original plant or vegetative division.

cutting – section of a plant removed for propagation.

deciduous – plants that lose their leaves annually – most usually in autumn or after the growing season.

die back – the browning and death of growth tips due to disease or frost.

diploid – a cell that contains twice the haploid number of chromosomes found in a gamete.

division – separation of a larger plant in smaller clumps usually during dormancy. Normally leaving at least two older pseudo-bulbs and one new or emerging growth.

epiphyte – plant that uses another to offer support without being a parasite.

epiphytic – pertaining to an epiphyte.

evergreen – plants that retain their leaves at the end of the growing season.

gene – part of the chromosome that controls hereditary characteristics.

genera – plural of genus.

genus – botanical collection of similar species.

grex – hybrids with the same parentage.

habitat – the natural environment of a plant.

haploid – cell containing only one representative from each pair of chromosomes.

hirsute – referring to the hairs on a stem, leaf or flower parts.

hybrid – resulting offspring derived from a crossing of two parents.

inflorescence – stem of flowers. (*See* panicle, raceme, and spike).

intergeneric – hybrid derived from different genera.

keiki – (pronounced *keekee)* from the Hawaiian word referring to an offshoot of a plant

lip – (labellum) modified petal.

lithophyte – orchid which usually or is naturally found growing on rocks or rocky outcrops.

lithophytic – referring to a lithophyte.

mericlone – plant reproduced from tissue of a mother or original plant and which is identical, i.e. vegetatively reproduced.

meristem – the growing stem apex used for vegetative propagation from a mother or original plant in order to multiply genetically identical plants. (*See* clone, mericlone).

monopodial – pertaining to a group of orchids which have a stem that grows annually from the apex.

mycorrhiza – a specific fungus which is required for successful germination of orchid seed.

node – point or knot on a stem.

ovary – female part of the flower which contains ovules and will eventually swell to a seed capsule.

panicle – refers to a branched stem or inflorescence.

peduncle – the stalk of a flowering head.

peat – a very fibrous material that is removed from the ground and usually broken up or left chunky and used in potting mixes. It is moisture retentive and acidic by nature.

peloric – pertains to an abnormal flower where one or more of the parts simulate another.

pendulous – usually referring to sprays of flowers that hang downwards.

picottee – refers to the naturally dark or light coloured edge of an orchid flower.

pH – scale on which acidity and alkalinity are measured.

pollination – the transfer of pollen to the stigma or stigmatic surface resulting in fertilization of embryonic seeds in the ovary.

pseudobulb – an often swollen storage organ of an orchid consisting of fibrous and fleshy matter. It exists above the soil or potting media level and emerges from one or more modified leaves.

raceme – an unbranched flowering stem.

root ball – roots and soil or potting media visible when an orchid or a plant is removed from a pot.

rosette – group of leaves that emerge usually at ground level from a short growing tip of a corm or underground bulb. Pertains to terrestrial orchids.

saprophytic – An orchid which is usually or naturally found growing on decaying organic matter and lacks green leaves.

sheath – covering of flower buds, especially Cattleyas.

species – population or populations of morphologically similar plants having common characteristics which separate them from other such groups.

sphagnum moss – mosses that are common to bogs and are water retentive.

spike – inflorescence in which flowers lack stalks.

sterile – infertile plant that cannot breed – often refers to triploids.

sympodial – term used for a group of orchids in which the new growth is a lateral shoot.

terrestrial – plants that naturally grow in the ground.

tetraploid – cell that contains four times the haploid number of chromosomes.

triploid – cell that contains three times the haploid number of chromosomes. Triploid plants are usually found to be sterile and will not breed.

vinicolour – deep wine red or burgundy colouration in flowers.

xanthotic – referring to yellow flowers.

PREVIOUS PAGES *Pot.* Cindy Yamamoto 'Crownfox' (Sally Taylor x San Damiano) AM/AOS.

CITES

By Dr Phillip Cribb

Most orchid growers immediately think that the major piece of conservation legislation protecting orchids in the wild is the Convention on International Trade in Endangered Species of Wild Fauna and Flora (CITES). However, this is a fallacy. CITES regulates international trade in orchids through a permitting system. In most countries, other laws have been passed that control orchid collection either at a local or national level or both. These are usually controls on collecting wild plants, for example, on private or public land, or in nature reserves or national parks. In many countries, such as Australia, South Africa, Solomon Islands and Papua New Guinea, controls exist at national, regional and local levels, and permits are required at each level for legitimate collecting to occur. CITES only comes into effect when plants are moved across international barriers.

CITES is an international treaty that was drafted at a meeting of 80 countries in 1973 when, as a result of the concern that uncontrolled international trade was endangering some species, such as tiger, rhinoceros and elephant, a United Nations meeting formulated a treaty to control such trade. It came into force on 1 July 1975. The entire orchid family was included at that time, mainly on the grounds that enforcement agencies could not be expected to differentiate threatened species from other orchids in their traded condition. At first, countries were slow to enact national legislation to bring CITES into effect. However, nowadays some 169 countries, including all of the orchid-rich ones, operate CITES. To do so, each country has to set up a Management and a Scientific Authority. Permits for the export of both wild and cultivated orchids can be applied for, and the Scientific Authority will advise the Management Authority on the status of the species and whether a licence should be granted or not. However, the decision to issue a permit lies solely with the Management Authority. The latter will certainly take into account whether specimens have been

A modern, well-maintained nursery selling Vanda hybrids.

Freshly jungle-collected plants are being established in this nursery.

collected under permit (legally acquired) if they are wild-collected. In some countries or blocks of countries, such as the European Union (a single market of 25 member States – where once CITES material has legally entered one member state it can freely move throughout the EU), a CITES import permit is also required. This can usually only be obtained if the importing Management Authority has had sight of an export permit.

All orchids are on CITES except for fermented, vanilla pods, orchid seeds and seedlings in flask, commercial cut flowers – such as those that can be purchased in the airports at Singapore and Bangkok – and artificially propagated orchid hybrids in the genera *Cymbidium*, *Dendrobium*, *Phalaenopsis* and *Vanda*, if they are packed to the standard laid down by CITES. There are three Appendices to CITES. Appendix I contains those species threatened with extinction. Less than 200 species of orchid are on Appendix I, including all slipper orchid species in the genera *Paphiopedilum* and *Phragmipedium*. Trade in effect is banned in wild specimens for commercial proposes – but artificially propagated material can be freely traded with the correct permits. All other orchid species are on Appendix II of CITES, while legitimately propagated material of Appendix I species are also treated as Appendix II plants. Appendix II includes all those species whose trade needs monitoring to prevent excessive exploitation leading to unsustainable utilization. Trade in both wild and artificially propagated plants of Appendix II specimens are allowed again subject to permit.

The orchid world has not reacted very positively to CITES, mainly because of its original blanket approach to all orchid trade. Furthermore, a great deal of misinformation has circulated among orchid growers about CITES. This has been compounded by stricter national controls in some countries. Some countries have, under their national legislation banned all exports of wild orchids; often they ban all exports of all wild plants. This is frequently misinterpreted to be a result of their implementation of CITES. It is not; it is merely the country putting in place strict national legislation – as is their sovereign right.

There has been significant movement within CITES to remove a wide range of artificially propagated orchids from its control. Such changes require a two-thirds voting majority of all the CITES countries present at a meeting of the CITES Conference of the Parties. Such changes are hard fought, and it is incumbent on orchid specialists and growers to ensure that their national delegations are fully briefed on such initiatives. Proposals can fail by just one vote.

In summary, CITES is one of many tools being utilized to make sure that orchid species do not become extinct in the wild. Its sphere is international trade and its remit does not extend to salvage or other national issues. It has produced a number of positive results, not least that it has heightened awareness of conservation issues in the orchid world and has led to a greatly increased production of artificially raised seedlings of species for the nursery trade. CITES cannot be wished away as some in the orchid fraternity have advocated; rather it is being continuously refined at each meeting of the Conference of the Parties (CoP), held biannually, to ensure that it fulfils its aims. Logical and well-balanced argument and lobbying of delegates, rather than denunciation, is the way forward for the orchid community in relation to CITES. It is important that such lobbying fits into the timetable of the countries' preparation for a CITES meeting, which normally starts some nine months before a meeting of the Conference of the Parties. Lobbying a national delegation just before they leave for a CITES CoP is likely to have a minimal effect, as the national position may already have been reached. Many countries are part of regional blocs that co-ordinate their positions – such as the European Union, the ASEAN countries or mega-diverse Latin American countries. Such groups meet early to consider their positions. To influence their decisions you must lobby them early with sound arguments. If you are meeting with senior officials or ministers, give them a maximum two-page clearly reasoned brief on your position, making it clear what the advantage is to their country from your proposal. Meeting a senior official or minister who has not had the opportunity to review your position and consult their national experts will just waste your time and theirs. If you set out on a mission to dissemble CITES you will fail; if you set out to craft it to work better for plants you will find many who will help you and you will be successful. CITES needs informed input and debate.

The increased training of customs and enforcement staff will also lead to increased targeting of illegal trade rather than picking up possible minor errors by the legitimate orchid trade, which is mostly concerned nowadays with artificially raised plants rather than wild-collected ones.

To keep up to date on CITES, check the CITES Secretariat website at www.cites.org. The European Union Wildlife Trade Regulations can be consulted at www.eu-wildlifetrade.org. You can follow the CITES negotiations at meetings of the Conference of the Parties and at the CITES Plants Committee by consulting the Earth Negotiations Bulletin at www.iisd.ca – the Bulletin tracks the major environmental negotiations as they happen, and there is also an extensive archive.

CONTACTS

CITES Secretariat
International Environment House
Chemin des Anémones
CH-1219 Châtelaine
Geneva, Switzerland
tel: +4122 917 8139 or 40
fax: +4122 797 3417
cites@unep.ch
www.cites.org

European Orchid Council
arachne@ludens.elte.hu
falco.elte.hu/eoc/EOC.htm

International Plant Names Index
www.ipni.org/index.html

International Register of orchid hybrids
see details for Royal Horticultural Society

Orchid Specialist group
//go.to/orchid-specialist-group

AUSTRALIA
Australian Orchid Council
www.orchidsaustralia.com

HOLLAND
De Nederlandse Orchideeën Vereniging
www.nov-orchidee.nl

UK
British Orchid Council
www.british-orchid-council.info

Royal Botanic Gardens, Kew
Richmond
Surrey
TW9 3AB
tel: +44 (0)20 8332 5000
fax: +44 (0)20 8332 5197
info@kew.org
www.rbgkew.org.uk

Royal Horticultural Society
Administrative Offices & General Enquiries
80 Vincent Square
London
SW1P 2PE
tel: +44 020 7834 4333
info@rhs.org.uk
membership@rhs.org.uk
www.rhs.org.uk

USA & CANADA
American Orchid Society
16700 AOS Lane
Delray Beach
FL 33446-4351
tel: +1 561 404 2000
fax: +1 561 404 2034 or 561 404 2100
TheAOS@aos.org

Canadian Orchid Congress
www.canadianorchidcongress.ca

SOUTH AFRICA
South African Orchid Council
www.saoc.co.za

INDEX

PHOTOGRAPHIC CREDITS

Copyright rests with the individuals and/or their agents listed below. Key: l = left; r = right; t = top; b = bottom; c = centre; tl = top left; tr = top right; bl = bottom left; br = bottom right; tc = top centre. (No abbreviation is given for pages with a single image, or pages on which all photographs are by a single photographer.)

p 1–5	Mike Tibbs	p 94–97	Mike Tibbs
p 6 l–r	Mike Tibbs; Mike Tibbs;	p 98–99	Roy Smith
	Phillip Cribb; Roy Smith	p 100–11	Mike Tibbs
p 7 l–r	Mike Tibbs	p 112	Martin von Fintel
p 8–11	Mike Tibbs	p 114	Mike Tibbs
p 16	Sam Field	p 115 tl, tr, br	Mike Tibbs
p 17 t	Mike Tibbs	p 115 bl	Roy Smith
p 17 b	Sam Field	p 116–18	Mike Tibbs
p 18–22	Mike Tibbs	p 119	Roy Smith
p 24	Sam Field	p 120–26	Mike Tibbs
p 25–26	Mike Tibbs	p 127	Roy Smith
p 27	Phillip Cribb	p 128	Greg Alikas
p 28–30	Mike Tibbs	p 129	Roy Smith
p 31	Roy Smith	p 130	Mike Tibbs
p 32–39	Mike Tibbs	p 131–32	Glen Decker
p 44	Carmen Coll	p 133 tl, tr	Glen Decker
p 45–51	Mike Tibbs	p 133 bl, br	Mike Tibbs
p 52–56	Sam Field	p 134	Greg Alikas
p 57 tl, tc, tr	Sam Field	p 135	RF Orchids
p 57 b	Mike Tibbs	p 137	Greg Alikas
p 58–75	Mike Tibbs	p 138–39	Mike Tibbs
p 78	Roy Smith	p 140	Greg Alikas
p 80–87	Mike Tibbs	p 141–42	Martin von Fintel
p 88–89	Roy Smith	p 144–47	Mike Tibbs
p 91–92	Mike Tibbs	p 150–51	Greg Alikas
p 93	Roy Smith	p 152–53	Mike Tibbs

AUTHOR'S ACKNOWLEDGEMENTS

I would like to dedicate this book to the memory of Allan and Sylvia Graham. Two dear orchid friends.

PUBLISHERS' ACKNOWLEDGEMENTS

The publishers wish to thank Joyce Monson for her invaluable contribution to this book, and Penny Brown for the index.